Life Lessons

from the Seniors of Vashon Island

Text by
John A. McCoy

Design by
Richard Rogers

Editing by
Alice Bloch

*To a meaningful and joyful life
for every older adult*

CONTENTS

Preface: How the book came about 5

Life Lessons indexed alphabetically 6

Seniors indexed by name and lesson 156

Acknowledgments 158

About the Author, Designer, and Editor 159

PREFACE

Over the past five years, I interviewed 135 seniors on Vashon Island, Washington, for "Life Lessons from Our Seniors," a semi-monthly column that appeared in the *Vashon-Maury Island Beachcomber*. The purpose of the column, sponsored by the Vashon Senior Center and two local businesses, was to share life lessons from our elders.

I interviewed seniors at the Senior Center, in their homes, in coffee shops, on park benches, and in library meeting rooms. During the height of the COVID-19 pandemic, I conducted interviews over the phone, on Zoom video, or masked outdoors six feet apart. Some seniors I asked for interviews declined ("I don't want to be in the paper"). Seven agreed to the interview but didn't want it published when they saw what I had written. But the overwhelming majority of interviewees were candid and forthcoming, willing to tell me about the good and the bad, the joyful and the sorrowful.

In all cases, I shared what I had written with the interviewee before it went to print, something I rarely did in my professional career as a journalist. As a result, I was able to correct errors and misrepresentations beforehand. It made the column better. In the cases where the interviewee insisted on her way or the highway, I took the highway and ditched the column.

The newspaper format of Life Lessons gave me about 350 words to tell a senior's story and draw out a lesson. "Brevity," as Shakespeare put it, "is the soul of wit."

Brevity meant condensing one to two hours of conversation to its essence. Who is this person? What propels him? What makes her tick? What singular lesson have they learned in 60, 70, 80, or 90 years of life that made a difference for them—and, perhaps, could make a difference for us?

That's what Life Lessons are about.

John A. McCoy
Vashon Island, Washington
June 2022

LIFE LESSONS

Accept people as they are 8

Adapt 9

Appreciate one another 10

Ask yourself: Why not? 11

Be a pioneer 12

Be adventurous 14

Be curious 15

Be flexible 16

Be generous 17

Be grateful 19

Be in the moment 20

Be of service 22

Be practical 23

Be quiet and listen 24

Be thankful 25

Be there for seniors 26

Be you 27

Be yourself 28

Be your own boss 29

Bid game 30

Breathe 31

Bring order 32

Care for others 33

Change is constant 34

Create 36

Delight in people 38

Discover your gift 39

Dive in 41

Do art 42

Do it while you can 43

Do it yourself 44

Do something about it 45

Do what brings joy 46

Do what you enjoy 47

Do what you love 48

Don't worry, just smile 49

Embrace opportunity 51

Embrace what comes 52

Enjoy people 53

Enjoy your health 54

Enjoy your work 55

Every day is a real prize 56

Expect the unexpected 57

Experience the arts 58

Experience the world 59

Faith is 'hands on' 60

Feed hungry kids 61

Figure it out 62

Find balance 63

Find the right partner 64

Find your calling 65

Find your love 66

Fix it 67

Get the facts 68

Give me a chance 69

Go for it 70

Go for what you want 71

Go to the woods 72

God has served me well 74

God provides 75

Heed the vulnerable 76

Help others 77

Help people 78

If it's broke, it's fixable 79

Include everyone 80

Innovate 81

It's your life 82
Jubilation 83
Jump in 84
Keep active 85
Keep moving 86
Keep on going 87
Learn through technology 88
Learning is for life 89
Let's talk about death 90
Life can turn on a dime 91
Live boldly 92
Live fully and intentionally 93
Make it better 94
Make something new 95
Mammals fascinate 96
Meet your neighbors 97
Mentor others 98
Offer a ride 99
Overperform 101
Pay attention 102
Persevere 103
Persist 104
Protect the earth 105
Prove your worth 106
Pursue stillness 107
Pursue your calling 108
Pursue your passion 109
Put family first 110
Read and learn 112
Read for happiness 113
Recognize opportunity 114
Recognize others 115

Reinvent yourself 116
Respect others 117
Ride horses 118
Say 'yes' 119
See the potential in others 121
See with new eyes 122
Seek contentment 124
Seek serenity 125
Seek understanding 126
Serendipity 127
Serve your community 128
Set goals 130
Share your passion 131
Stay put 132
Start over 133
Step up and do something 134
Take risks 135
Talk less, listen more 136
Teach, learn, eat local 138
Teamwork 139
Think freely 141
Travel opens eyes 142
Trust a friend 144
Try new things 145
Unlock the trauma 146
Use a personal touch 148
Walk and reflect 149
Welcome change 150
Work can be satisfying 151
Work hard 153
Work together and things happen . . 154
Write 155

ACCEPT PEOPLE AS THEY ARE
Sigrid Thomas

Sigrid Thomas met her second husband when both were cast in a Drama Dock production of *One Flew Over the Cuckoo's Nest*. She played Nurse Ratched, the tyrannical nurse who is the main antagonist.

"And then I took care of him ever afterward," she jokes.

Sigrid, a member of the Senior Center's Fun and Funds Committee and a regular volunteer at the front desk, is not a natural Nurse Ratched. She's a warm, gregarious, good listener who accepts people as they are. "I don't try to argue people into anything," she says. "I just enjoy them."

Born in Tacoma, the daughter of a teacher and a homemaker, Sigrid is one of six sisters and a sole brother, who became a Lutheran minister. She had a happy childhood. She graduated from Wilson High School and went on to Washington State, where, she says, she "got an M.R.S. degree." She and her first husband had two children and lived in nearly a dozen states until the marriage foundered.

In 1979, Sigrid and her children moved to Vashon, where she volunteered to be a stage manager for Drama Dock. Yet she and her ex-husband remained close. When she planned to marry Dean Thomas, her acting partner, the ex and his girlfriend came from Texas to bless the union.

After a stint as a waitress, Sigrid worked for 23 years as the receptionist for the late Dr. Charles Weispfenning, an island MD who championed alternative medicine. She chuckles, recalling his remedy for plantar warts: duct tape.

In a home near the Senior Center, Sigrid raised her children and took care of her father and her ailing husband, who died in 1997. Recently, she bought a second house in Fircrest so she could be next door to two of her sisters. In many ways, she figures, she's gone full circle.

I don't try to argue people into anything; I just enjoy them.

ADAPT
Chuck Hoffman

Chuck Hoffman, a retired state mental health administrator, doesn't wince at being called a "government bureaucrat." Fresh out of college, he oversaw patients in the geriatric psych ward of what was then the biggest mental institution in Illinois. Thirty-six years later, he retired as a network manager for Illinois mental health services and moved to Vashon.

Like most states, Illinois was de-institutionalizing, discharging mental patients into the community. The theory was that group homes and local mental health centers could provide less costly and more effective treatment than massive, walled institutions. Implementing that theory consumed Chuck's career.

He was the oldest of three boys raised in a comfortable, middle-class Lutheran home in the Chicago suburb of Mt. Prospect. Dad was an office manager for International Paper; mom, a medical records clerk. Chuck attended the Lutheran grammar school and graduated from public high school. Inspired by his father's love of literature, he earned a BA and MA in English at Northern Illinois U, where he managed to live in a frat house without joining the frat.

In a French class, he fell for Linda Picher, who was engaged to a guy in college in Iowa. When the boyfriend came to visit her, Chuck loaned him his car. The visit ended with Linda dumping her fiancé, losing Chuck's car, and starting a new romance with Chuck. They married a year later.

Setting aside his English degrees, Chuck found a job at the Illinois state mental hospital in Elgin, followed by another at a mental health facility in New Hampshire, and, when he and Linda returned to Illinois, re-employment at Elgin. A subsequent MSW through the University of Illinois put him on an administrative track with the state Department of Mental Health. Over the following years, he helped set criteria and monitor community treatment programs. He administered grants to reduce homelessness, establish housing with social services, and place the mentally ill in homelike settings.

Even-tempered and adaptable, Chuck was good at coordinating and carrying out policy. He brought those skills to the boards of the Vashon Senior Center and Vashon Youth and Family Services. "Finding the balance," he calls it.

Chuck Hoffman began his long career as a mental health administrator at the massive state hospital in Elgin, Illinois.

APPRECIATE ONE ANOTHER
Mary Tuel

Until *The Loop*, Vashon's alternative newspaper, folded in 2021, Mary Tuel wrote a semi-monthly column titled "Spiritual Smart Aleck." She liked the antithesis: spirituality with cheekiness. As she explained in one column, "I am a Christian with a potty mouth and sick sense of humor. I try to behave, but if anyone needs Jesus, it's me."

The second of two children born to a resourceful apple farmer and an erratic homemaker, Mary grew up in Watsonville, California. A quiet, dreamy child, she wrote stories about horses, learned piano and guitar, and sang. How she loved to sing! At three, she recorded "O Come All Ye Faithful" with her dad. She majored in journalism at Cal Poly, San Luis Obispo, but left with her lead guitar boyfriend to be a rock 'n' roll star in LA. She peddled herself as a singer-songwriter but, ultimately, was back in Watsonville with mom and dad.

Still the music throbbed in her soul. "Music was everything to me," Mary says. A fiddler from her rock/country band got her to come to Vashon to be the "chick singer in a new band." So, Mary drove her '58 Chevy to the island in a January snowstorm and moved into a hippie pad. Her room was a mattress at the top of the stairs. Six years later, after a couple of unwise relationships, she married Rick, a fellow musician, and had two sons. It was a good marriage, lived entirely in the rehabbed mess hall of a church camp. Mary sang and played guitar in the trio, Women, Women & Song, "a house band for middle-aged ladies." Rick, a water worker, died in 2013.

He appears frequently in Mary's columns, which tackle subjects ranging from feral cats to rodeo cowgirls (her college roommates) to politicians being "thrown under the bus." Her writing is candid, funny, and reflective. "The isolation of the pandemic," she writes, "taught me how fragile and precious we are to one another."

After cancer surgery and a fall that broke her vertebra, Mary is realistic about the future. Friends — islanders she's known for half a century — are dying and "that sucks," she says. "Gratitude, deep breathing, and prayer get me through. Prayer connects me with them and the Creator."

Mary Tuel performs at the 1975 Vashon Strawberry Festival.

ASK YOURSELF: WHY NOT?
Ted Clabaugh

You could bookend Ted Clabaugh's career with two old buildings: 1) a rundown Los Angeles hotel whose small rooms were occupied by lonely and isolated seniors; and 2) a failing Vashon nursing home whose residents were about to be evicted.

In 1963, fresh out of Harvard Law School, Ted rented a tiny seventh-floor room in that LA hotel because the California bar exam course was conducted in the basement. He noticed the other tenants had no visitors or family. For them, the holidays were particularly dreadful. So Ted asked himself: Why not do something? His question led to an annual charitable effort that resulted in free holiday dinners for tenants of LA's Skid Row hotels.

In 1995, his law practice now on Vashon, Ted and his wife Vicki were the first to stand up at a community meeting to pledge $10,000 toward a $300,000 loan guarantee that saved the nursing home, transforming it into the nonprofit Vashon Community Care. It was called the "Christmas Miracle." Ted served as VCC Board president for eight years.

The only son of a government chemist and a homemaker, Ted grew up in Arlington, Virginia. He loved to read. In third grade, he read 131 books, many of them histories about colonial Virginia and the Founding Fathers. At the University of Maryland, he majored in political science and got involved in student government. He regards the Declaration of Independence and the US Constitution as "incredible" documents for their wisdom and eloquence. In part, those founding documents led him to law school.

A slender, affable fellow who remains an avid reader, Ted practiced law for 24 years in the LA area: litigation, business formation, trusts, probate, corporate mergers and acquisitions. But in 1987, tired of the LA scene, he and Vicki discovered Vashon, which reminded Ted of his bucolic childhood summer cabin on Chesapeake Bay. They moved to the island and Ted hung out his shingle. He retired in 2016.

Ted Clabaugh, left, at the grand opening of the Vashon Community Care Center in 2001.

BE A PIONEER
Tanya Roberts

Tanya Roberts' life has been "adventuresome." When her mother sent her off to preschool, Tanya sallied forth without looking back. Her mother cried. In high school she avoided study hall by persuading the librarian to let her play chess with a friend. At the University of Washington, when her PhD advisor insisted on his economic modeling assumptions, Tanya moved to New York City and became a printmaker. "I'm a pioneer, a wild woman and a Unitarian," she laughs.

The oldest of four children born to a geologist and a homemaker/artist, Tanya grew up in a Federal Way home that was alive with curiosity, science, and music. Each family member accompanied mom on the piano with a different instrument. Tanya played clarinet. "Those were the happiest times," she says.

She did well in school, excelling in debate and math, but didn't take kindly to being told woodshop and trigonometry were for boys. At the UW, she fell in love with microeconomics and married an econ student. The first love lasted; the second didn't. In NYC, Tanya soon abandoned printmaking and returned to "applied economics." She liked solving real-world problems. She taught, compiled labor statistics, assisted a nonprofit, and, while completing her PhD, wrote a report for the US Senate on dairy safety regulations.

In 1977, she landed a job with the Dept. of Agriculture in Washington, DC, researching food safety policy. She became an expert on estimating the costs to society of foodborne illness. The job was very fulfilling, says Tanya. "I had lots of autonomy and worked with all these scientists." At a Christmas party, she met Paul Kolenbrander, a microbiologist who studied mouth bugs. After testing their relationship on a 24/7 trip to Japan, she agreed to marry him. Why? "I found out he listened to me."

The couple worked in DC until retirement in 2009. Two of Tanya's childhood friends enticed them to resettle on Vashon. Paul passed away in 2017, but Tanya remains active in causes ranging from anti-racism to food safety. In fact, she gave a Friday talk at the Senior Center titled "The Political Economy of Antibiotics in Animal Feed."

Tanya Roberts, 14, plays clarinet accompanied by brother Brian, 12, on trombone,
sister Janine, 10, on violin, and brother Mark, 5, seeking donations in 1957.

BE ADVENTUROUS
Harriet Nelson

Harriet Nelson, who taught hundreds of grade school kids in Auburn, was a very creative instructor. As an exercise in geography and culture, she had her sixth graders study airline schedules and tourist brochures and then write letters home imagining they were in London, Paris, and Rome. One boy took the lesson so seriously that his distressed mother phoned Harriet to ask: "Is David really going to Europe tomorrow?"

In Harriet's classes, students wrote a play in Spanish, staged a Japanese sukiyaki dinner, and imitated a Native American potlatch in which they all gave gifts to each other.

"I loved teaching," says Harriet, a joyful, optimistic woman who had expected to retire in 1991 together with her first husband, also a teacher. She and Howard Shull, whom she met at Pacific Lutheran University, had raised three kids in Puyallup. Now they were looking forward to spending some of their senior years in the Tahlequah cabin that Harriet's dad had built in the 1930s with lumber floated across from Tacoma. But Howard died, and Harriet was bereft.

On Valentine's Day 2002, at the invitation of a friend, Harriet attended a reunion in Yuma, AZ, of graduates of Tacoma high schools. She had gone to Stadium; Rich Nelson had gone to Lincoln; and under the Arizona sky that night, they fell in love. Rich, a widower, phoned her soon after and asked her to marry him in the cathedral in Bergen, Norway, on June 2. Harriet agreed.

Harriet Nelson, at 85, prepares for a parachute jump as husband Rich points out how far she will fall.

You see, when opportunities arise, Harriet rarely hesitates. She's whizzed across ziplines. She parachuted at age 85. She's traveled on every continent except Antarctica. She and Rich's busy lives gravitate between a winter home in Arizona, the cabin on Vashon, his relatives in Montana, and their kids' lives around the Northwest. As a result, they belong to four Lutheran churches and contribute to each of them. "It's so important to stay involved," Harriet says.

BE CURIOUS
Deena Eber

Deena Eber was a sheltered, privileged, 15-year-old city girl when a friend drove her to Mt. Baldy in the Angeles National Forest. As the car climbed into the wilderness, she spotted two idyllic log cabins tucked in the woods. She was enchanted. She wondered how people lived in such a remote, beautiful place.

That wonder transformed Deena's life. She realized she didn't have to live in Los Angeles, didn't have to copy the lives of others, and was absolutely free to pursue her own path. "I'm really a curious person," says Deena, a petite, upbeat woman who teaches tai chi at the Senior Center. "I want to see who people are and how they live."

> *I got from life so much more than I ever expected.*

The child of a sales entrepreneur and a homemaker, Deena grew up in Beverly Hills but dropped out of college. It was the '60s and a lot was happening outside the classroom. Deena fell in love, married, and had a son. When the marriage unraveled, she and son David hit the road. They lived on beaches in California and Hawaii, in the woods near Mt. Shasta, and in the New England countryside. Deena did bookkeeping and odd jobs, such as sewing buttons on moccasins.

But as a poor, single mother with an eight-year-old, she knew she had no future. She went back to LA and school. She graduated summa cum laude and became a CPA. Yet it was people—not tax accounting—that intrigued her. Deena, who had clipped classified ads for friends, was offered a position as a corporate headhunter. Bingo!, she soon recognized. This is it.

In 1989, she opened a headhunting office in Bellevue while working for a national executive recruiting firm. Three years later she started her own executive recruiting business at Seattle's One Union Square. The business took off. Her clients included Microsoft, Amazon, and other big names. In 1997, she and her cats moved to Vashon. "I got from life so much more than I ever expected," she says.

BE FLEXIBLE
Dick Vanderpool

Let's call Dick Vanderpool "flexible." The Seattle native was 11 when his mother died. His widowed father, a freight manager, recruited relatives to help raise Dick and two younger sisters. By the time Dick graduated from Queen Anne High School, he had a Union Oil summer job, a '35 Plymouth, and a scholarship to Linfield College in Oregon.

Dick thought he'd become a transportation manager. At college, however, he found his math wanting and switched to history. A train ride altered his life. Enroute to a national student assembly, Dick met Nancy shortly after she boarded at The Dalles. Three nights later they were dancing in a New Year's Eve ballroom in Lawrence, Kansas. The romance continued as both returned to college and then Dick got drafted.

He did two years in the Army at Fort Ord, California. Nancy finished college, they got engaged, and she won a graduate assistantship to Syracuse University. Although he had no teaching experience, Dick thought, "I better find a teaching job in New York." He borrowed his dad's credit card, bought a '50 Plymouth, and slept in it as he drove across the country. A village 165 miles from Syracuse hired him to teach New York State history to seventh graders. He and Nancy married and, until she completed her degree, he was a weekend husband.

Nancy got a job at Penn State, so Dick enrolled there as a graduate student. He began a PhD dissertation on Warren G. Harding, which eventually led to an appointment as a history prof at Northern Montana College. This time Nancy followed him.

Years later, with both wanting to return to the coast, it was Dick's turn to be flexible. Nancy took a top post at Oregon State University in Corvallis. And Dick became the entire history department at a community college in Roseburg, 99 miles down I-5. He did a weekly commute for 16 years until both retired and moved to Vashon. "Life has its tradeoffs," Dick says without complaint. "I've been fortunate."

Life has its tradeoffs.
I've been fortunate.

BE GENEROUS
Anne Tuttle

Anne Tuttle has an indelible childhood memory of her father, a C&O Railway man, sending hobos up the hill to the family home in Clifton Forge, Virginia, to have her mom get them a cup of coffee and something to eat. It was the Depression. Yet Anne, her parents, and five siblings had chickens, a big vegetable garden, and food aplenty. So much that dad gave away the surplus to their Allegheny Mountain neighbors.

"I learned early," says Anne, a sparkly, fun-loving widow of 91, "to be kind and generous in helping others."

At home, her mom made the kids' clothes, including a green velvet evening dress for Anne to wear at a Christmas dance. (Anne's granddaughter, 62 years later, wore it to the prom.) In high school, Anne discovered a talent for drawing and painting. She did cartoons and posters and postcard sketches for the Presbyterian Men's Bible Class (her first paying job). Her forte, however, was social life. Her senior class of 43 students voted her "most popular" and "wittiest."

After graduation, Anne enrolled in a recreational leadership program in Richmond, Virginia. "It was right down my alley," she says, "puppetry, folk dancing, camping, and games." At church she met Bob Tuttle, a University of Virginia student. Their first two dates were not promising. Bob took Anne to watch a boxing match and later invited her to shoot beer cans with a .22 rifle. "But, you know," she says, laughing, "we really hit it off."

They married in 1952, and Bob did four years as a Navy pilot, followed by 33 years flying for Pan American and United Airlines. He, Anne, and their four kids lived on both coasts and in Berlin, where Anne introduced their German neighbors to Bingo. After Bob retired, their three daughters convinced them to move to Vashon. For years, Anne and Bob volunteered to assist cancer patients coming to the Fred Hutchinson Center in Seattle. With her sweet Virginia accent, she specialized in making patients from the South feel right at home. Today she is "the social director" of Vashon's Meals on Wheels, phoning homebound seniors to arrange lunch deliveries.

"I have to have a project," explains Anne, who spent the pandemic painting watercolor postcards she sent to friends. "I've been so fortunate; I want to give back."

*Ann Tuttle and her husband, Bob, a commercial pilot for Pan American
and United Airlines, sit in the cockpit of a Boeing 727.*

BE GRATEFUL
Wally Fletcher

Wally Fletcher was a 59-year-old corporate executive when he got his Lexus and drove the perimeter of the United States. He camped in national parks, sleeping under the stars. When he returned, he quit paid work forever. "Life was too precious to be tied up with job pressure and commitments," recalls Wally, a tall, imposing fellow with a mane of white hair.

So the man who had once been responsible for hundreds of subordinates and a million-dollar budget at Pitney Bowes, became an activist and a crisis interventionist. Shortly after 9-11, he was at a healing service at St. Mark's Cathedral when a distraught woman approached the communion rail and told him: "I'm going to kill myself today."

He made a deal with her. "Phone me before you kill yourself," he said. A few hours later, she called. He took her for a long walk and she told him her story. She'd lost her boyfriend, her job, her savings, and now, depressed and abandoned, she couldn't face returning home to Philadelphia. Wally arranged for his daughter, who lived in Philly, to meet her at the airport. He and the woman kept in touch and, within months, her life had turned around. "You buy time until hope comes again," Wally explains.

A Connecticut Yankee most of his life, Wally was single when he moved to Kirkland in 1991 to be near one of his three children. In 2005, he relocated to Vashon, where his dog, Thor, could enjoy the outdoors. One day, the two of them discovered the Senior Center.

"The Center became a focus of my life," says Wally, who participates in everything from lunch to lectures to watercolor painting. A baritone, he also sings in the Island Chorale, leads "Music Mends Minds" at Vashon Community Care, worships with the Episcopalians, and meditates with the Buddhists.

"I'm grateful every morning I wake up not dead," Wally rejoices. "Ha."

I'm grateful every morning
I wake up not dead.

BE IN THE MOMENT
Lindsay Hofman

Dana and Lindsay Hofman were newlyweds in San Francisco, where he was selling art at Fisherman's Wharf and she was completing a PhD thesis in biochemistry. And they were ready for an adventure. "Let's build a boat and sail away," Dana suggested. Lindsay, whose 52-year marriage to Dana ended with his death last year, said, "Yes."

They moved to Seattle, bought a house, and built a 44-foot trimaran in the backyard. It took seven years, during which Lindsay worked at the Mason Clinic, became a board-certified clinical chemist, gave birth to two boys, and taught biochemistry to women in Saudi Arabia. But finally, with two toddlers in tow, she and Dana set sail for Mexico.

The eldest of four children born to a US Foreign Service officer and a strong-minded mother, Lindsay embraced the world. Her father's assignments took the family to Moscow, Boston, Iowa, Washington DC, and Bangladesh, where she was sent off to a private boarding school in the Himalayan foothills. The tall, shy, studious girl who had preferred riding horses to socializing, made many lifelong friends. And discovered chemistry.

"I love the structures in chemistry—the way molecules react," says Lindsay, visibly brightening. She earned her BA in science at Smith College and a PhD in biochemistry at the University of Washington, where she fell for Dana, an undergrad art student, during Mountaineers ski lessons.

After their family sailing adventure, Lindsay and Dana returned to Seattle broke. She took a clinical chemistry position with a lab, developing tests to screen newborns for disease. They lived in a small house in the Vashon woods with acreage for horses, ducks, and chickens. When North Carolina asked her to run the state's newborn screening lab, she and Dana were off to Raleigh for six years. When a Vancouver, Washington lab called, promising a job developing saliva tests, Lindsay thought: Why not? And thus, she and Dana were soon back on Vashon. She later opened her own saliva testing lab in Pioneer Square. "Looking back," concludes Lindsay, who retired in 2017, "I was always living in the present."

Lindsay Hofman, her husband, Dana, and their boys, Gordon and Pierce, at sail on their trimaran off Cabo San Lucas in 1980.

BE OF SERVICE
Bob Spangler

The middle child of a five-and-dime store manager and a homemaker, Bob Spangler grew up a straight arrow in McKeesport, Pennsylvania. He was a good student, an Eagle Scout, and a "nerd" whose best friends called themselves "the Crazy Eights." His parents encouraged him to go to Davidson College, then an all-male Presbyterian school in North Carolina. After two years, though, he wanted to be closer to home and to girls.

That summer he set out on a solitary road trip by train, bus, and thumb. He worked in pea-processing plants in Walla Walla and Pendleton and journeyed to California. Returning home, he transferred to Penn State, determined to be a lawyer. The next summer he volunteered to tutor poor kids at a Presbyterian mission station in Puerto Rico. "There I cemented my affinity with the church," he says. "I saw it in action."

Service to others is fundamental.

Bob graduated in economics and went to law school at Duke. But the ROTC commitment he made at Penn State was due. The Army commissioned him a second lieutenant and, in 1968, assigned him to a military intelligence unit in Vietnam. "The war was a life-defining experience," says Bob, who had a hard time reconciling what he saw with his core Christian beliefs. "I lived day by day, hoping to get out alive."

After discharge, Bob reclaimed a job he'd had at the Federal Communications Commission in Washington, DC. It was an exciting time. The government broke up AT&T, regulated cellular service, and dealt with the Internet. One day he met Carol, now his wife of 50 years, in the elevator of their DC apartment building. They married in 1970, bought a house in the planned community of Columbia, Maryland, had a girl and a boy, and lived there until moving to Vashon in 2005 to be closer to family.

On the island, Bob volunteered at church and at Vashon Community Care, where he was Board secretary. Twice a month now he and Carol wait in an RV parked outside the Tacoma Detention Center to help released immigrants make travel plans and arrange housing. "Service to others," Bob says, "is fundamental."

BE PRACTICAL
Lars Strandberg

About every six years Lars Strandberg returns to Jakobstad, the little town on the Finnish coast that he left as an eight-year-old when his family set out for America. He has "Finn-Swede" cousins there and, on one trip, was attempting to manage his way in the Swedish he'd learned as a boy. A cousin gently suggested he opt for English—they'd understand him better.

But even in English, some things are lost in communication. Lars, a retired pharmacist, was interviewed by the local paper on that trip. The reporter, missing the distinction between a druggist and a drug dealer, quoted Lars as saying, "I do drugs."

Early in life, Lars was convinced that he should pursue something practical. His parents had worked too hard and suffered too much in Finland and later in Olympia for him to fritter away an education. His dad worked variously as a small hotel operator, grocer, and carpenter, while his mother toiled as a laundress and seamstress. Lars, their younger son, could speak so little English on arrival in Olympia that he was held back two years in school. As a result, he was the only student who drove a car to junior high.

Eventually, he finished high school, spent a year at Washington State, then transferred to the University of Washington to complete a degree in pharmacy. "I knew I'd have a job," he says. And he did. Lars plunged into "institutional pharmacy," providing medications and health supplies to nursing homes, care facilities, and prisons.

For 30 years Lars and several partners operated institutional pharmacies in Seattle, Tukwila, and Port Orchard. At one point they had 80-plus employees. Ultimately, Lars got burnt out on late night emergency calls and having to "deal with corporate America 24/7." He sold it all and, in 2000, began work behind the counter at Vashon Pharmacy. He loved it. He had time for tennis, the garden, wife Annie, his daughters and grandkids. It was so practical.

At eight, Lars Strandberg and his family emigrated from a Swedish-speaking community in Finland.

23

BE QUIET AND LISTEN
John Moore

John Moore, a skilled occupational therapist, was midway through his career in the US Army when he learned a valuable lesson: Be quiet and listen. A slender, forthright, retired colonel, John designed custom braces and modifications to prosthetics for wounded soldiers at military hospitals. One of his creations was an artificial hand and forearm wrapped in camouflage so that a determined infantry sergeant could use his weapon again and return to battle.

John discovered, however, that his ingenuity in patching up injured soldiers was not enough. While stationed at Madigan Hospital in Tacoma, he did graduate work in guidance and counseling and awakened to the emotional and psychological needs of his wounded warriors. "I learned to shut up and listen," he says.

Born in Connecticut, John spent his teen years fishing for swordfish off Martha's Vineyard. By the time he completed a degree in occupational therapy at the University of New Hampshire, he had married Brenda, and the first of their two boys was on the way. The Army offered him a commission and an internship in occupational therapy.

A retired Army colonel and occupational therapist, John Moore carves spoons.

So from 1963 until 1990, John helped severely injured soldiers survive and recover. At the height of the Vietnam War, he was working at a US evacuation hospital in Japan that was receiving 100 troops a day. "The guys who made it," he says, "maintained a positive attitude and never gave up."

After the Army, John and Brenda moved to Vashon and built a home on Dockton Heights. For a few years, he worked in the orthopedic department at Group Health. After retiring for good in 1999, he joined the Rotary, served on the Senior Center Board, and took up a new avocation: whittling spoons from what he calls "second chance" wood. You can see his handiwork at the Vashon Farmers Market.

BE THANKFUL
Carl Coldeen

You wouldn't think that Carl Coldeen would be a thankful fellow. He was born with cerebral palsy, an incurable disorder that has affected his coordination, speech, and muscle movement. He wears hearing aids and has a home phone equipped with a screen that turns a caller's words into text. Since his mother's death several years ago, he has lived alone.

"Some people don't want to deal with people with cerebral palsy," says Carl, a happy fellow who delights in a good joke, a humorous story, or a stimulating conversation. "I don't care. I'm just grateful to be alive."

The good Lord provided me with everything that I need, and everything has worked out fine.

The oldest of four children born to a sheet metal worker and a homemaker, Carl moved with his family from Spokane to Seattle when his dad got a job at Boeing. When Carl was 16, his folks bought a house on Westside Highway, where he has lived ever since. He graduated from Vashon High School and worked for more than a decade at Beall's Greenhouses where he sprayed roses for mildew. But he developed severe allergies and had to quit. Later he found temporary work as a caretaker at the Sportsmen's Club, but ultimately, he was forced to apply for disability.

Still, Carl wanted to do something. Hitchhiking on the main highway one day in 1982, he got a lift from his old high school principal, who suggested Carl check out the Senior Center. At 36, Carl was hardly a senior. No matter, he fit in perfectly. "I like old people," he says. "I like old people a lot."

Ever since, Carl has volunteered at the Center. He sets up lunch tables, puts out the silverware, and serves the noon meal. He also does the settings for birthday parties, special lunches, and celebrations. And he tends to numerous small tasks that keep the place running smoothly. "The good Lord provided me with everything that I need," Carl says. "And everything has worked out fine."

BE THERE FOR SENIORS
Rain Sheehan

At age 22, Rain Sheehan is hardly a senior. Yet she has spent more time with seniors than many people do in a lifetime.

A bubbly, cheerful person who calls herself "a nerd and a knowledge enthusiast," Rain credits her love of seniors to her maternal grandfather, Al Zumbrun, who died when she was 16. Grandpa Al lived in a cabin attached to the family home in the woods near Camp Sealth. With her parents divorced, no siblings, and her single mom working, Rain says Grandpa was "absolutely my best friend." An "unconditional-love type of guy," he drove her to school, handed out donuts to the carpool kids, taught her poker and baseball, and gave her a zest for life. A Navy submariner in World War II, he went ashore within days of the atomic bomb blast at Nagasaki. The experience transformed him. He told Rain he saw no justification for war or nuclear weapons.

After his death, Rain walked into Vashon Community Care and told a manager, "I want a job around old people." She had finished her high school work at 15 and was taking online college courses in neuroscience, astrobiology, and poetry. VCC was impressed, started her as a housekeeper, and was soon paying her way to become a certified nursing assistant.

Four years later, Rain continues to help VCC residents eat, bathe, dress, and handle medications. She treats them as friends, teasing and entertaining them with greetings such as "Good morning, princess." And, when the final time comes, she sees them through it. She once sat 14 hours straight with a dying woman so that her exhausted, elderly husband — who didn't want her to die alone — could take a break. When he returned, his wife passed away.

On Wednesdays from 3 to 5, Rain hurries from VCC to the Senior Center, where she helps folks who have issues with their smartphones and laptops. Her computer clinic is drop-in and free. And, Rain figures, another opportunity to be with seniors.

Grandpa was absolutely my best friend. An unconditional-love type of guy.

BE YOU
Daphne Purpus

Daphne Ashling Purpus, a name she created for herself, wears a safety pin just above her heart. The message is: I'm a safe person and this is a safe place. It's a message to "outliers" like herself, especially the scores of nonconforming students who come to her for help with math—and life.

"For many years I did my best to fit in," says Daphne, who describes herself as an introvert with an anxiety disorder. "It didn't work. I was depressed and desperate."

Moving to Vashon in 2006 saved her. Daphne found the house she wanted—one story, compact, secluded—and painted it purple. Inside she did the rooms in rainbow colors and lined the walls with fabric bolts from which she makes quilts she calls "portable hugs." Here she writes haiku poetry and magical fantasy novels (11 published so far) and enjoys the company of Wilson, her dog, and four cats. Recently she built a "catio," an enclosed catwalk with way stations that encircles the outside of the house.

The oldest of three girls, Daphne grew up in the LA area, the daughter of two English professors. At five, she witnessed her mother die in a house fire. A smart and serious student, she graduated from Pasadena Polytechnic High School and earned a physics degree at UC Davis. Later she completed degrees in library science, English, and Latin. She wrote a PhD dissertation on how Scottish medieval historians viewed King Arthur.

Yet Daphne felt duty bound to conform. During the Vietnam War, she became a naval officer, married another naval officer assigned to the Great Lakes Naval Training Center, and had a daughter and son. For 20 years she tried to be a "Donna Reed homemaker" but failed, finally ending her marriage.

Daphne and her teenage son moved to Arizona where, at age 52, she says, "I realized I was a lesbian." After reading an article citing Seattle as the country's No. 1 lesbian city, she moved again and lived in several Seattle neighborhoods, but nothing fit. Then she discovered Vashon. "It was perfect for me," Daphne recalls, "beautiful, gay-friendly, and a bit weird. I was finally home."

Daphne Purpus encircled her house with an enclosed catwalk – a "catio."

BE YOURSELF
Reva Sparkes

Reva Sparkes was two-thirds through life when she realized she was happy with herself. It was her 60th birthday. Surrounded by her colleagues at a Chinese university, she was pulling cooked noodles out of a large bowl. Her noodles were long, very long. "You'll have a long life," her fellow teachers said, "a very long life."

Reflecting on that moment, Reva says, "I decided I wanted to be who I started out to be."

Direct and down-to-earth, Reva was one of five children born to a Grange supply store manager and a homemaker in Dayton, Washington. She graduated from the local high school and then earned a teaching degree at Eastern Washington College. "I taught sixth grade for one miserable year in Sprague," she recalls. "The kids didn't want to be there and neither did I."

She switched to social work, arranging adoptions in Spokane and later managing vocational rehabilitation services in California and Oregon. Along the way, she got married three times. "God knows why," she says.

In Eugene, she met Kate, a woman who had a home on Vashon and would become her partner for life. "It was Kate's determination, not mine, that got us hooked up," Reva says. So in 1980, she and her two children, a boy and a girl, moved to the island to be with Kate. Life was good. Reva and Kate traveled the world, looked up Reva's relatives in the UK, and wrote "Bingo Sisters," a gossip column for Bingo Bugle.

It was Kate who found the advertisement seeking English teachers in China and urged Reva to apply. So off she went for a "wonderful" year with the Chinese. Although Kate died a decade ago, Reva remains active. She volunteers at the Senior Center, where she exercises regularly and plays bridge, pinochle, and bingo. "I live each day as it comes," she says.

BE YOUR OWN BOSS
Don Lofstrom

Over an up-and-down career in truck stop management, financial fuel services, computer systems, and prefabricated home construction, Don Lofstrom concluded: Be your own boss.

The younger son of an Exxon sales executive and a homemaker, Don grew up in New Jersey forced to play basketball because he was a lanky 6'3". He hated it and took up the bass guitar, becoming good enough to open for the Dave Clark Five. He started university at Clemson, with a shaved head and mandatory ROTC, but finished at Lafayette College, where he was DKE fraternity president. With graduation, he and Marge, his new bride, were off to Las Cruces, New Mexico, where Don earned an MBA.

He quit his first job — arranging home loans for the city's low-income residents — when his supervisor rewarded his good work with a nickel-an-hour raise. He became a truck stop manager at quadruple the pay. The trucking industry moved him and his family to bigger jobs in Illinois, Tennessee, and Rochester, New York, where he became CFO of a spinoff financial fuel services company. He had 80 employees and made good money but was putting in 60-100 hours a week. And then, boom, it was over. Venture capitalists scooped up the business and showed him the door.

Now in Nashville, where Marge had a secure teaching job, Don sent out 130 resumes. He got a job as a parts manager for a computer store, only to discover that the owner was stealing the merchandise and the business was bankrupt. He and three other ex-employees founded "Phoenix," a computer services firm "rising from the ashes."

Still, Don hankered to go it alone. He cashed out his Phoenix shares and bought the Lindal prefab cedar home dealership for Tennessee. He sold the homes, hired the crews, and supervised the construction. "It gave me great satisfaction," he says. So much so, that he did it until he and Marge retired and moved to Vashon in 2016.

It gave me great satisfaction.

BID GAME
Carol Butler

In bridge, as in life, Carol Butler likes to "bid game." She has made decisions—majoring in French, compiling a dictionary of Romanian slang, becoming a lawyer (inspired, at age 10, by Perry Mason), and moving to Micronesia to represent indigenous people against the US Government—that many might regard as impractical and foolhardy. "They're not rational decisions," she concedes. "If you rationalize, you'll never go for it."

The youngest of four children born to the first chairman of the Washington State entomology department and the secretary of the botany department, Carol grew up in Pullman in a home that prized learning. Although her parents divorced when she was four, the siblings remained close to each other and their parents. Carol excelled in school and had a social life centered on church and extracurriculars. She was a Camp Fire Girl, in 4-H, drama, and debate. At Pullman High School, she played the lead role in *The Diary of Anne Frank*.

Carol went on to the University of Washington, but the frequent protests, the drugs, and the campus chaos put her off. She transferred to Middlebury College, a small Vermont school where she received a BA in French. She went on to earn an MA in

Carol Butler, who won a Fulbright to Romania, in the dress she wore to a village Easter festival in 1973.

French at Tulane. And then, curious about Romanian, the romance language everyone ignores, she won a Fulbright Fellowship to study it in communist Romania. For a year and a half, she traveled around the country talking to provincial university professors about Romanian slang, something the Party claimed didn't exist. But, over coffee and cognac, the lists of slang came out.

When her Fulbright concluded, Carol returned to Tulane to realize her childhood dream of being a lawyer. In New Orleans she met George Butler, another law student, and, after both passed the Louisiana bar, they daringly took off for legal services jobs in Micronesia, then US-administered tropical islands in the mid-Pacific. "Our job," Carol says, "was to help return lands confiscated by Japan during World War II."

The couple married and in 1983 moved to Guam, where they practiced law and had three kids. With the kids grown, they retired in 2008 and decided to try life on another island. Carol's sister-in-law introduced them to Vashon, a great place to bid game.

BREATHE
Bob Hawkins

Bob Hawkins grew up so anxious that he couldn't concentrate on anything. Not at home in the Burien area. Not at school. Not in a succession of unsatisfying jobs that he muddled through.

Life at home was a "nightmare." His father, a hardworking house contractor, was driven, demanding, and critical. His mother, who did the books for dad's business, was depressed and withdrawn. His younger brother, his only sibling, had muscular dystrophy and died at 18. In the early years, his father's practice was to put the family in a basement, construct a house above them, sell the house when it was done and start over again. During grade school, Bob lived in three successive basements.

At Highline High School, he was a mediocre student who escaped into the outdoors backpacking with the Boy Scouts. He enrolled at the University of Washington but his heart wasn't in it. In 1964, a Boeing connection gave him a free seat to Europe on a plane delivery. He took it. He hitchhiked, Eurailed, and youth-hosteled around the continent. He discovered another world.

Revitalized by the European experience, Bob returned to the UW and completed a BA in English. He and a woman he married too quickly took off with another couple on a cross-country trip. In a poor Kentucky mountain hamlet with intermittent electricity, Bob and his bride stopped traveling and settled in. He taught high school but, ultimately, she left. "I didn't have it together," Bob concedes.

Back home in Seattle, Bob met Betty Kopp, a high school math teacher, on a blind date and fell in love. Overcoming her parents' disapproval of a divorced son-in-law, they married at St. Mark's Cathedral, which became their church home for 25 years. Bob again returned to the UW, now a motivated student in a master's program in psychotherapy. He finished the degree, rented a sixth-floor downtown office and began adult counseling.

He treated what he had suffered: anxiety, depression, neglect, obsessive self-criticism, and other conditions that rob people of satisfaction and joy. Still practicing, Bob asks clients to begin by breathing with whatever they are feeling.

Bob Hawkins rests at the high point of the UK's South West Coast Path.

BRING ORDER
Tink Campbell

Tink Campbell, whose Christian name is "Marilyn," was nicknamed "Tink" while she was still in the womb. No, it's not short for "Tinkerbelle" and has nothing to do with "tinkering." It's a rural Alabama endearment for "the little stinker."

The older of two children born to two Southern schoolteachers, Tink grew up bringing order to a fast-changing life. Her dad left teaching for a chemist job with the Atomic Energy Commission and later ran plants for Dow Chemical and International Paper. As a result, says Tink, "we were corporate gypsies." They moved from Alabama to Kentucky to Louisiana to Michigan, where Tink graduated from Midland High School.

It was more chaos than I needed.

At the University of Michigan, she studied political science and embraced the spirt of the 1970s. Sophomore year, she left the dorm to join a socialist cooperative in which residents shared meals, cleaning, and governance. Her dad dubbed it "an intentional slum community," Tink laughs. "It was more chaos than I needed." The following year she opted for a one-bedroom apartment.

After graduation, Tink floundered a bit through odd jobs, including handling subscriptions for the Michigan Mathematical Journal. And then she met Steve Benowitz at a three-couple dinner for which she did the cooking. The lights went out, and she and Steve talked all night. Magic happened. She moved with him to Columbus and then Cleveland, where they married in 1975.

In her work career, Tink tried to bring order out of chaos. In Cleveland, she supervised daycare homes, introducing every pre-K book she could find in the library. She then moved to Child Protective Services, a burnout job helping single mothers burdened by abuse, poverty, and unwanted children.

When Steve transferred to Washington, DC, Tink took a data processing course at a community college and began a second career as a software programmer. She wrote code and provided tech support, helping customers bring order to their data. When retirement beckoned, she and Steve knew they wanted to live in the Puget Sound area. Why Vashon? In part because a 10-year-old Tink had read the *Reader's Digest* version of island author Betty MacDonald's *Onions in the Stew*.

CARE FOR OTHERS
Zoe Bennington

One occupation runs through Zoe Bennington's life: bookkeeping. "There's no gray area in bookkeeping," she says, "it's all black and white — the numbers have to line up."

While bookkeeping is the constant, Zoe has done more than study spreadsheets. She's bartended, taught aerobics, and, during the height of the AIDS crisis in the 1980s, volunteered countless hours at the Whitman Walker Clinic in Washington, DC. There she cared for several friends dying of AIDS. And she and her best friend opened "Work It," a gym that served as a refuge for people who felt unwelcome elsewhere.

The gym also made her a better athlete. She did the AIDS Bike Ride from Philly to DC. She competed in 5K and 10k runs, mini-triathlons, and, in 1996, was an Olympic torchbearer to the Atlanta Games. "I don't define myself by what I do for a living," Zoe explains, "but by what I try to do for other people." She became an emergency foster parent, taking in at-risk kids so their mothers could have a break. When one of her two boys brought home a Korean child with no family in the US, Zoe took him in and became his guardian.

She was born British, the second of four children, raised by an electrical engineer and an English teacher, parents she describes as wonderful "socialist hippies." The family emigrated to Pittsburgh when she was six, moved to Virginia, then spent two years in Hong Kong before returning to the US, where Zoe graduated from high school in San Francisco. College was not for her, and she plunged into the working world in DC. After closing the gym, she started her own full-time bookkeeping business. She married, had two biracial sons, divorced, and, at age 57, married Steve Hildreth, a congressional defense expert.

When he retired in 2018, the couple, her three boys, and Steve's youngest daughter began a new life on Vashon. Zoe was soon on the island boards of Women Hold the Key and the Senior Center. Under her Badass Brands, LLC, she sells handmade salts, honey from her apiary, and "30+ years of experience keeping your books tight."

Zoe Bennington carries the flaming torch at the 1996 Olympic Games in Atlanta.

CHANGE IS CONSTANT
Richard Nagler

In those magnificent years before the Internet, Richard Nagler and his fellow librarians thought of themselves "as the guardians of the information universe." They held the key to all that knowledge arrayed in card catalogues, deposited in archives, and shelved in periodicals and books. With the arrival of digital technology, however, information moved from cards, microfiche, and books to electronic databases. Why ask the reference librarian when you can Google it?

After nearly 50 years as a librarian, Richard found himself freeing up paper jams on the copier and teaching computer research to students whose main interest was Facebook. Libraries became community centers with Internet access. A witty, scholarly, self-described "newspaper junkie," Richard missed the glory days. "Savor them," he says, "because change is coming."

Change came early in Richard's life. The Nazis sent his parents, Polish Jews, to a slave labor camp near Munich. His father died in an Allied bombing raid. After the war ended, a Jewish refugee resettlement agency brought him and his mother to New York City. She found a job as a lab tech at Mt. Sinai Hospital, and Richard went through middle school in Spanish Harlem. The two of them moved to Ann Arbor when she got a public health job at the University of Michigan.

At 15, Richard was shelving books at the city library. He worked there as he completed a political science degree at UM. He started law school but it was the 1960s and a big world beckoned. He went to San Francisco to work in a bookstore, then to New York City to another bookstore, then back home, where mom asked: "What are you doing with your life?"

Richard decided on a graduate degree in library science and became a lifelong librarian in Detroit and its suburbs. "I loved being a depository of knowledge," he jokes wryly. Along the way, he married fellow librarian Mary Anne Sergott, raised two girls, and when retirement came, discovered Vashon. Neither daughter became a librarian.

*Richard Nagler, a Detroit public librarian, staffs a
1970s information booth on the "Library of the Future."*

CREATE
Penny Grist

A constant in Penny Grist's life has been creating things that please the eye and move the spirit. Her love for art started with a sewing class. First she made clothing. Next it was jewelry. She has a memory of soldering jewelry on a humid, 98-degree day in her brownstone in New York City and saying to herself, "This is so beautiful and I'm so happy."

Failing eyesight eventually forced Penny to abandon jewelry making. But there was plenty of other art to create. She painted in water colors. She constructed furniture and made sculptures. She did mosaics and wove yarn baskets. "There's always something that captures my fancy," Penny says, "and I learn how to do it."

The oldest of three children, Penny grew up in Philly and New York City. Her father was a car mechanic who went on to be the computer hardware chief at the Time & Life Building in midtown Manhattan. Her stepmother, a war correspondent, was "one of the most interesting women I ever knew." Penny graduated from Penn State with a BA in General Arts & Sciences. "I'm a generalist," she says.

Fresh out of college, she got a job in the picture department at Time Life pasting labels on photos. She moved on to photo and then editorial research, delving into subjects ranging from cooking to history to current events and meeting fascinating people from all over the world. She married a banker, restored a Brooklyn brownstone, had a daughter, and divorced. On her first trip west in 1972, she fell in love with Seattle and Larry Muir, her husband of 44 years. They repaired a dilapidated house above Quartermaster Harbor and have lived there ever since. Penny was co-founder and director of Vashon Allied Arts, launching its art auction and garden tour. She taught painting and ran the Blue Heron Art Gallery.

For years musicians gathered in her art studio to share food, drink, and live music. Penny was the percussionist. She delights in folks coming together and enjoying each other's company. Once COVID ends, she plans to resume her hootenanny, she says. "I want a party every Sunday for the rest of my life."

Penny Grist, her cat Daisy, and husband, Larry Muir, make music in their art studio.

DELIGHT IN PEOPLE
Luella Lodahl

Luella Lodahl, a happy, spirited, bright-eyed lady who turned 100 in 2017, attributes her long life to other people. "I like to be with them and to help them if I can," she says. "And I like to smile."

Born Luella Riley in Kansas City, Kansas, she was a middle child. She likes to tell the story that her older sister was her mom's favorite and she was her dad's favorite until a third child was born. Their new baby brother then became everyone's favorite.

Luella was still a child when her family moved from Kansas to West Seattle. She attended West Seattle High School, where she tried to do her best. But really, she preferred church, which gave her an opportunity to hear music and sing. And, boy, did she love music, song, and dance.

During her high school years, you could find Luella and friends just about every Friday and Saturday night dancing to big band music at the Olympic Heights Club. It was there that she fell in love with Victor Lodahl, her husband-to-be.

Was Victor a good dancer?

"You bet he was," Luella replied, "or I wouldn't have been interested."

Luella and Victor married in 1935. She was just 18. Over the years, they became the proud parents of two girls, two boys, and an adopted son. And still they found time to dance, an activity that delighted their children, who loved to watch.

Not long after their marriage, Luella and Victor moved to Vashon. Victor wanted his children to grow up in a healthy, rural community and Luella agreed. She settled in as a homemaker and mother. She remembers those first years on the island as among the happiest times of her life. She raised her kids, babysat others' kids, and taught Sunday school.

"Education is so important," she tells young people today. "Stay in school and get a university degree if you can afford it."

A widow, Luella finds her friends today at the Senior Center. She enjoys the mid-day lunch and plays pinochle on Tuesday afternoons. She knows all the regulars and introduces herself to newcomers. "I like people," she says.

Education is so important.
Stay in school and get a degree.

DISCOVER YOUR GIFT
Brian Brown

Brian Brown was lucky. Early in life he discovered that he had an aptitude for editing. Yes, he could write. He especially enjoyed writing humor. But it was reorganizing a story, finding the missing element, or updating it that he was particularly good at. "I was a damn good rewrite man," Brian says.

Born in the Bronx and raised in affluent Scarsdale, New York, Brian was the middle child of an electrical engineer and a homemaker. Years later his friend Frank McCourt, the author of the Pulitzer Prize-winning *Angela's Ashes*, the tragicomic memoir of a wretched Irish childhood, told him he ought to write a book. "But I grew up in middle-class comfort and my parents loved me," Brian objected. McCourt had a title for him: *A Happy Childhood in Search of Misery*.

At his all-boys Catholic high school, Brian wrote a humor column that evolved into satire at St. Francis University, where he earned a BA. He freelanced for various newspapers while completing an MA in American Literature at NYU and hanging out with beatniks in Greenwich Village coffee houses. He wooed and wed Sheila Quinlan, a social worker, by reciting passages from Jack Kerouac's *On the Road* while they strolled Jones Beach.

The newlyweds moved to Indianapolis, where Brian progressed from UPI correspondent to news documentary director at WFBM-TV. They were soon back in the Big Apple, however, after *Time* magazine hired Brian as education editor. He covered "teach-ins" at universities, reported from the war zone in Northern Ireland, edited sci fi author Isaac Asimov, and was editorial liaison to Henry Kissinger for book excerpts in *Time*.

He and Sheila raised their four children in a Manhattan apartment where they lived for half a century. In 2007, following their kids west, the couple moved to Vashon, where Brian hosted "Brown Briefly," a weekly KVSH Radio current events show "where less is more, more or less."

Brian Brown, standing upper right, with the "Brieflies," participants in his current events show on KVSH radio. From left to right, Bruce Haulman, Kevin Jones, Lynn Carrigan, Truman O'Brien, Michael Shook, seated, Brown, and Susan McCabe.

DIVE IN
Barb Gustafson

Twenty-two years ago, Barb Gustafson, her husband Rick, and their two kids discovered Vashon on a ferry ride. It reminded Barb of her childhood home of Wrentham, Massachusetts, a close-knit lakeside community where folks left their doors unlocked and kids played in the woods. After a decade of moving around for Rick's job, she told him this is home. He agreed. He had a new position in Seattle, but she had no job and knew no one on the island.

So, as Barb does, she dove in. Schooled as a marine biologist, she volunteered to run the annual Science Fair at McMurray Middle School. She organized "Walk on the Wildside" outdoor learning for the library and the Land Trust. She led the baseline water quality testing and salmon counting in Shinglemill Creek. And for two decades she was the science enrichment teacher at Family Link, the school district's alternative learning program.

Creative and energetic, Barb taught without a textbook, making every lesson unique. She carted in tubs full of minerals, plants, bones, maps, instruments, charts, and microscopes and challenged students to dig in. "Hands-on science, that's what I did," she says. "Science is about engagement, observation, coming up with a question, and testing it. It's a lot of fun."

The third of four children born to a mechanical engineer and a science teacher, Barb had "a glorious childhood" with the freedom to explore. Her mother, an avid community volunteer, was her role model. Barb pursued gymnastics in high school and marine science at the University of Maine, where she fell in love with invertebrates and Rick, then a grad student studying clams. They married and headed to Victoria, BC, the first of his several post-doctorate stops.

No matter the place, Barb did science. On Vashon, she continues to teach math concepts to middle-schoolers through basket weaving. At the Vashon Bookshop, where she works part-time, she's the science expert. Look there for her photo book, *Vashon ABCs: An Exploration of Shore Life*. And, at the Senior Center, she's the armchair traveler, projecting and explaining nature photos from around the world.

Barb Gustafson and ecology summer campers do water quality testing at Fisher Pond.

DO ART
Geri Peterson

Geri Peterson was a management instructor at Boeing when her sister-in-law signed her up for a watercolor class. "You gotta be kidding," Geri exclaimed. "You want me to do art?" But at the very first class, she was hooked. "I could not believe how much fun it was." Five months later she sold her first painting. And for more than a decade she has taught a watercolor class at the Senior Center.

"You can't make a mistake in watercolors," says Geri, an ebullient great-grandmother who delights in her students. "You can always paint over."

The only daughter of a US Army officer and a homemaker, she was on the first transport ship to Japan after World War II ended. The family lived in a Quonset hut. After her dad's service, they settled in Skagit County, where Geri graduated from Sedro Woolley High School. She married her high school sweetheart and had three kids. A logging injury disabled her husband and ended their marriage. Geri needed a full-time job fast. The unemployment office sent her to wash dishes at a huge Boeing cafeteria in Seattle.

At Boeing, Geri rose fast from dishwasher to cashier to secretary to head clerk for mockup planning on the 737. She learned to read blueprints and create production plans. Upgraded to "manufacturing engineer," she was one of only three women among 800 men with that job title. Her home life improved. On New Year's Day 1970, Geri met Jack, a divorced father of five, in Skykomish as both prepared to ski at nearby Steven's Pass. "We were the only people in town without a hangover," she laughs. "At the top of the chair lift, he asked me out." They married and bought a home on Vashon.

After 32 years at Boeing, Geri retired, planning to teach art. She earned a teaching degree at Pacific Lutheran University and got a job at Stadium High School. It was tough. Drugs, delinquency, disruptive students, poor administrative support. Jack told her, "Stay home and do art." She took his advice.

You can't make a mistake in watercolors; you can always paint over.

DO IT WHILE YOU CAN
Betty Hawkins

The only daughter and the middle child of a Navy chaplain who became a Presbyterian pastor, Betty Hawkins came from a very strict home where the rules and expectations were clear: Mom tends the home; Dad rules the roost. Church on Sunday. Prayer at meals. No movies or dancing. And "limited dating."

Betty, studious, bright-eyed, and good natured, went along with it. At Yakima High School, where she was class secretary and a member of the Honor Society, she volunteered to help in the principal's office. Later, at Wheaton College, where she was active in Youth for Christ, she earned a BA in math and a teaching credential. She returned to Yakima and settled into what appeared to be a conventional career as a math teacher, first in Yakima and later in Kirkland. Not so.

She went off to an Asian studies program in Japan, lived on Lake Union, and met a recently divorced man on a blind date. Betty married Bob and the two of them did things that she'd never done before: skiing, backpacking, self-guided walking trips in Italy, Britain, France, Turkey. She did summer teaching in Nigeria and medical mission work in the Amazon. She won a National Science Foundation grant, earned an MA at Rutgers and specialized in teaching math to women and inner city kids.

Betty and Bob's first home was a historic Ellsworth Storey cottage built in 1905 in the woods off Seattle's Lake Washington Blvd. They paid $50 a month for 540 square feet. When the first of their two sons started to walk, it got too small and they eventually bought a house on Capitol Hill, where they lived for 23 years. Betty commuted to Shoreline Community College to teach math. Nearing retirement, she responded to a realtor's call about a beach bungalow in Dockton, came over, and made an offer. The deal was done before Bob even saw it. They have happily lived there ever since.

Today Betty is confined to a wheelchair, the result of a neurological disorder akin to Parkinson's disease. Her mobility is limited and her memory fading. Yet she remains upbeat and attentive. "I did it while I could."

Betty Hawkins trekking at 10,000 feet in the Italian Alps.

DO IT YOURSELF
Gary Peterson

Forty years ago, Gary Peterson started building the two-story, 2,200 square-foot house that he and his wife, Linda, occupy on Vashon. While handy with tools, he was not an experienced carpenter. He'd been a radiation safety expert at Lawrence Radiation Laboratory, the nation's premier nuclear weapons laboratory, and a scientific systems analyst at Boeing. He quit the lab, convinced radiation levels were unsafe. He quit Boeing, convinced that with the time, money, and stress of commuting to Seattle, he'd be better off self-employed.

Gary designed and built the house, relying on "how-to" books and "math, geometry, and physics." His materials "were inexpensive, readily available, and long-lasting." The roof is concrete, the siding vinyl, the deck unpainted fir. Twelve solar-heated fiberglass tubes, filled with thousands of gallons of water, rise to the ceiling behind south-facing windows. They cool in summer, heat in winter. Gary paid material costs with side jobs making furniture, rehabbing houses, and restoring historic buildings.

The older of two sons, Gary grew up in "crushing poverty" in rural Minnesota. His childhood home was a renovated chicken coop across the street from the Jolly Green Giant processing plant in Le Sueur, population 3,000. He and his brother shot

Gary Peterson built 12 solar-heated, water-filled fiberglass tubes to heat his home in winter and cool it in summer.

squirrels, rabbits, and pheasants to put meat on the table. His parents, with eighth-grade educations, struggled through a series of menial jobs. Gary credits their decision to move 10 miles south to St. Peter, a college town, for transforming his life.

An eighth grader at the time, he was thrust into a bigger, more engaging world. He did well in high school math and science ("it's clear, cut, and dried"), graduated with honors, and commuted to Mankato State where he earned degrees in math and physics. The Atomic Energy Commission awarded him a graduate fellowship to the University of Kansas, which resulted in the laboratory job.

Any regrets about abandoning physics for carpentry? None, says Gary. "We're lucky. We're debt-free. We raised our three sons and now we give back." One giveback is the ice skates that he and Linda provide at Fisher Pond whenever it freezes over.

DO SOMETHING ABOUT IT
Al Slaughter

Al Slaughter, who turned 90 in 2017, has done a lot of things in life, many of them unexpected. When Al, a tall, athletic guy who enjoys a good story, sees a need, he does something about it.

As a result, he's been a delivery boy, ferry deck hand, naval officer, merchant seaman, realtor, Rotarian, furniture store owner, community activist, volunteer fire captain, fire commissioner, driver's ed instructor, and water district president. He once appeased King County by persuading the Clam Clove Water District to replace their dodgy reservoir. "I had the brilliant idea to put in a well," he says, chuckling.

Born in Seattle and raised in Oregon and Tacoma, Al moved to Vashon in 1943, when his folks bought nine acres near the Tahlequah ferry dock. An only child, he attended Vashon High School while helping staff his father's furniture store in Tacoma. He graduated from Vashon and completed a business degree at the University of Puget Sound. In 1954, he met Carol at a YMCA singles party, married her in 1955, and moved with her to his parents' island property in 1957. They've lived there ever since.

They've raised two children, a boy and a girl, and "nearly every animal ever created," including chickens, ducks, rabbits, pigs, cows, goats, sheep, pigeons, and guinea hens. They've had fruit trees and a large garden. "We tried to be self-sustaining," Al explains.

When Al got the novel idea of putting the South End Community Center and the Tahlequah fire station into one building, he went to Olympia to argue before the state attorney general. No fire district had ever before leased space from a community group. He prevailed.

Now a great-grandfather, Al is a bit surprised that he has dwelt in the same place for 74 years. But hey, if you're content, love Vashon, and have something to do, why go elsewhere?

Al and Carol Slaughter look out from the South End Community Clubhouse, closed in 2012.

DO WHAT BRINGS JOY
Marge Beardsley

In Marge Beardsley's 91 years, there was really just one man: Jim Beardsley. Their marriage began the year she graduated from the University of Washington and lasted until his death in 2013. Sixty-one years. And there were really just two homes. The one in West Seattle where she and her three siblings grew up in comfort and contentment, and the one on Vashon where she and Jim raised four kids and she still lives today—69 years later. But, boy oh boy, there were sure a lot of horses.

Marge, who started riding at age five and had her first horse at 10, figures that over the years as many as 100 horses have been stabled and ridden on her westside acreage. A half-dozen, tended and trained by her daughter, live there now. An oil painting of Captain, a big, handsome gelding who was her favorite, hangs in the living room hallway. "Being outdoors, working with a horse, riding and grooming it," Marge says, "it's so satisfying."

While Jim commuted to the family-owned industrial fabrication company in West Seattle, Marge tended to the kids and the horses. She taught horsemanship to her own children and, through the US Pony Club, to scores of other young riders. They learned dressage, show jumping, and cross-country riding. For a time, she was the US Pony Club's regional supervisor, responsible for 34 clubs in five states.

An oil painting of Captain, Marge Beardsley's favorite horse, hangs in her hallway.

Her passion for horses came from her own childhood experience riding in the Olympic Mountains. Every August her family would saddle up their horses with food, tents, and camping gear for two weeks of trail riding. "We'd be up there in the mountains and never see another soul," Marge recalls. On one occasion, without horse trailers available on the island, they rode their steeds from home right onto the ferry boat to Southworth.

On doctor's orders, Marge stopped riding horses at age 65. But her home remains a magnet for kids, grandkids, and their friends who come to ride, swim, or explore the beach. Marge is active at the Senior Center, where she plays bridge and volunteers. And when folks there ask her about horses, she beams.

DO WHAT YOU ENJOY
Jan Perry

In eighth grade, Jan Perry wanted to be a home economics teacher. She liked school, she admired her teachers, and, in a time of career limitations for women, teaching was something she would enjoy just fine. So, for 37 years she taught high school home economics. "My life has been a straight line," says Jan, an affable extrovert. "I liked teaching and I like people."

She is the oldest of seven children born into a Catholic family in Chelsea, Michigan, a town known as the home of Jiffy Mix. Her mom was a homemaker while dad, a cost estimator for a machine company, also worked as an electrician and realtor. It was a happy childhood with loving parenting and clear expectations. "My dad hoped we would go to college," Jan says, "but at a state school with in-state tuition."

She enrolled at nearby Michigan State, a university with 10 times the population of Chelsea, and lived in the dorms. She graduated with a teaching degree and, at her dad's insistence, had a job nailed down before heading off on a summer adventure at Glacier National Park. At age 21, Jan was teaching home economics, speech, and debate at little Portland (Michigan) High School, where "some of the seniors looked older than me."

Her time in Michigan ended after she married a fellow MSU grad who took a horticulture job at then-thriving Beall's Greenhouses on Vashon. The couple bought a house in Burton, and Jan soon had a home economics position at the high school. Over the years, the job expanded from sewing, food, and cooking into health education. She taught about human sexuality, addiction, and mental illness to both girls and boys. In total, she figures she had nearly 10,000 students, some of whom — decades later — still address her as "Mrs. Perry."

At age 60, Jan retired from teaching. Single, she moved to a condo in town, did volunteer respite care, served on the Vashon Scholarship Foundation, and began work at Vashon Pharmacy. She's there now two or three days a week, helping customers and catching up with former students. "Call me 'Jan,'" she says.

Jan Perry, with her ex-students Carl Fox and Chantel Uto, now coworkers at Vashon Pharmacy.

DO WHAT YOU LOVE
Joe Bryan

At age three, Joe Bryan knew he was a scientist. He asked questions all the time. He took apart appliances that his father, a mechanical engineer who became a dairy farmer, brought home to repair. "I was good at fixing things," he says. In grade school, he built crystal radio sets. His father and mother, a librarian, schooled their four children in learning.

Life on their 150-acre dairy farm near Slippery Rock, Pennsylvania, was hard. Joe milked two dozen cows and rode a bus an hour each way to high school. There was little time for extracurriculars. He delved into math and physics. At a reunion 50 years later, his classmates remembered him as "the nerd."

He won a scholarship to the Rensselaer Polytechnic Institute (RPI) in Troy, New York, where a night job as a hospital orderly led to training as a lab tech. He thought, "I'll be a doctor." He completed his BS in physics at RPI and won admission to an MD-PhD program at the University of Pennsylvania. While in medical school he married for the first time, had a daughter, and became convinced by a class in cell biology that he'd be a better scientist than physician. "I'm a physical, mathematical, quantitative guy," Joe says. Adds Lydia Aguilar, his wife, "Joe cares more about molecules than people."

Post-graduate work at the Woods Hole, UC Berkeley, and UW Friday Harbor Laboratories followed. Joe returned to Penn to teach cell and molecular biology before moving to the Baylor College of Medicine in Houston in 1978 to work on cell division.

Dr. Joe Bryan and his scientific colleague and wife, Dr. Lydia Aguilar, study an x-ray transparency in their lab at the Baylor College of Medicine.

In 1979 he met Lydia, developing a lasting friendship that led to marriage in 1985 and a daughter in 1988. It proved a perfect professional match: Lydia was a medical doctor with a PhD in genetic epidemiology. At Baylor, the two immersed themselves in diabetes research identifying molecules important for control of insulin secretion. In 2007 they moved to the Pacific Northwest Diabetes Research Institute in Seattle. By the time they retired on Vashon in 2018, they had done more than 60 years of genetic research on diabetes. Why? "Because we loved it," Joe says.

DON'T WORRY, JUST SMILE
Bernie O'Malley

Bernie O'Malley helps out. He dressed as a holiday Elf to solicit funds for Vashon Youth and Family Services. He served on the boards of the Vashon Island Growers Association and the Senior Center. He paired up with community activist Hilary Emmer to run on a Bernie-Hilary ticket for honorary Mayor of Vashon. They won, raising $6,000 for the Senior Center.

Typically dressed in a straw hat, floral shirt, and shorts, Bernie operates the weekend produce stand in front of The Hardware Store restaurant. In season, he and his crew truck fresh fruits and vegetables from small farms in the Yakima and Puyallup Valleys and sell them alongside Vashon produce. Cherries, blueberries, peaches, corn, cucumbers, lettuce, etc., all freshly picked.

Raised in Detroit and a graduate of the University of Michigan, Bernie never expected to be selling veggies on an island in Puget Sound. "You can't know what will show up or why," he says, "so don't worry about it."

As a youth, Bernie worked for storekeepers, many of them immigrants who taught him the art of selling. On a trip west in 1972, he discovered Vashon, was enchanted by its beauty, and determined that he would live here. He found a job managing a consumer cooperative in Kirkland. There he fell in love with Norine Grace, a single mother of two, and they married in 1977.

In 1990, they moved to the island and built a home on Dilworth Road where they planted thousands of flowers, especially dahlias. When both of them retired from the Seattle Water Department, they created a dahlia flower business and established the produce stand. Norine passed away in 2017.

But Bernie soldiers on. He has fruit and veggies to sell. A cart to drive in the Strawberry Festival Parade. And more funds to raise for worthy causes.

Community activists Bernie O'Malley and Hilary Emmer win the 2016-17 campaign for Vashon's unofficial mayors on a Bernie-Hilary ticket.

EMBRACE OPPORTUNITY
Lydia Aguilar

No one would have predicted that Lydia Aguilar, a Mexico City physician and genetic epidemiologist, would retire to Vashon and become the radio voice of the Latino community and a key member of the island's volunteer Medical Reserve Corps responding to the COVID pandemic.

Her father was a lawyer, publisher, and economics professor with a lifelong commitment to social justice activism. Her mother was the daughter of Russian Jews who immigrated to the US and started over with nothing. "They had a wonderful marriage," says Lydia, whose mother spoke Spanish with a Brooklyn accent.

Lydia and her older brother grew up in the bohemian district of Coyoacán with music, books, galleries, and a cultural elite that included artists Diego Rivera, Frida Kahlo, and David Alfaro Siqueiros. From age four, Lydia was determined to be a physician and help as many people as she could.

She received her MD from the National University after six years of study, then did a three-year hospital residency. Along the way, she developed an interest in the genetic component of chronic diseases, particularly diabetes, which afflicted members of her family. Her genetics mentor encouraged her to pursue graduate work in the US, where she enrolled at the University of Texas School of Public Health in Houston. Lydia's PhD research focused on identifying genetic markers for diabetes in a Mexican-American population in south Texas and provided free diabetes screening, physical exams, and diabetes education.

In September 1985 a massive magnitude-8.0 earthquake struck Mexico City, leveling buildings, cutting off communications, and killing over 5,000 people. Joe Bryan, a scientific colleague and dear friend, flew to Mexico to find Lydia. When he did, he proposed marriage. Lydia agreed. "It's easier to find a good job than a good partner," she says.

Returning to Houston, the newlyweds began their diabetes research at the Baylor College of Medicine and had a daughter. In 2007 they took diabetes research positions in Seattle and moved to Vashon. Three years ago, Lydia began "Mi Gente Latina," her Spanish-language show of public health, island news, and Latin American music on Voice of Vashon.

Lydia Aguilar conducts diabetes research in her lab in Seattle.

EMBRACE WHAT COMES
Ellen Trout

Ellen Trout describes herself as "very sequential." She has been a school teacher, an education consultant, and co-owner of a hardware store and, later, a cruise-only agency. To all these jobs, Ellen has brought good planning, attentive listening, and practical solutions that bring people together. Cheerful and positive by nature, she makes the best of the hand she's dealt.

Ellen was eight when her parents moved the family from Michigan to Kent, where she was a member of the first class to attend Kent-Meridian High School. She went on to earn education degrees at Washington State and Central Washington. For the next 30 years she taught children from kindergarten through junior high in Longview, Kent, and Federal Way. She loved teaching and demonstrated it. The school district had her mentor newer teachers who needed help.

Some things are beyond our control; just embrace what comes next!

Meanwhile, she married and had two children. In 1971, while she was still teaching, she and her husband opened a Coast-to-Coast hardware store in Federal Way. She taught by day and did the books at night. When they lost the lease in 1986, they began the cruise agency, the first in the Northwest. In 1988, Ellen retired from teaching and devoted herself full-time to the agency. It had its perks: cruises all over the world.

But then came the Internet and people could book their own travel. And then came 9-11 and people were fearful of traveling. Both the business and the marriage ended.

Yet Ellen, optimistic as ever, moved on. In 2004 she came to Vashon to be near her daughter, son, and four grandchildren. Ellen joined the Senior Center to play bridge and was soon teaching the game to others. She was invited to serve on the Center's Board and was elected president.

"Some things are beyond our control," she says, with a smile and a shrug. "Just embrace what comes next!"

ENJOY PEOPLE
Barb Stoddard

One of the memorable cases that Barb Stoddard handled as a paralegal involved an intoxicated partygoer who lay down in the middle of a Tacoma street. He got run over by another partygoer who then accidentally backed the car over him. "He was pretty well damaged," Barb recalls, "but he survived." Both partygoers happened to be insured by State Farm, which meant that Barb's lawyer boss, who represented State Farm, had a delicate situation. He wanted to avoid going to court by achieving a settlement to which both partygoers would agree. Barb interviewed them as well as a witness in the car.

"I like people," she says, smiling at the thought of that peculiar case, "and I like asking difficult questions." The case was settled. Both sides accepted 50 percent liability.

I like people, and I like asking difficult questions.

A merry widow who makes the jello shots for the Senior Center's Rainbow Bingo, Barb grew up in Seattle's Rainier Valley, the only child of a jazz trumpeter and a tap dancer. She was a student at the University of Washington when she met Paul Stoddard, a Coast Guardsman and a third-generation Islander, on the ferry Klahowya. She was 19; he was 20; and it was "pretty much love at first sight." They married within the year, moved to Vashon, and bought his parents' home on the Maury Island heights where she has lived ever since. (Paul died in 2008.)

The couple raised three daughters. When the girls were teens, Barb returned to school and became a paralegal. When she retired in 2000, she volunteered as a court-appointed special advocate for children: "a very rewarding experience."

Last year Barb was diagnosed with a rare, life-threatening autoimmune disease that left her hands and feet numb. With better medicine, she is recovering and is optimistic about further improvement. She gets help with walking from Addison, her five-year-old great-granddaughter. "She puts her hands on my hips to help me turn," Barb says, laughing.

ENJOY YOUR HEALTH
Betty Beymer

In her nearly nine decades of life, Betty Beymer counts herself fortunate to have had a long and successful marriage, loving children and grandchildren, enjoyable employment, and, until she lost her vision, good health.

"I never thought I'd lose my eyesight," says Betty, an active, sociable woman who now depends on audiobooks from the library, large-print bridge and pinochle cards, and her daughter's help to read her email. "It's not a lot of fun watching the Seahawks with my nose pressed to the TV."

Yet Betty tries to concentrate on the good. There are a lot of good memories. Born in Tacoma, she was seven when her family of five moved to Burton. Her dad, an auto mechanic, ran the nearby gas station and garage. At 17, Betty graduated from Vashon High and immediately married Dick Beymer, who was 21. The marriage lasted until his death 68 years later.

"It was a good decision," Betty recalls fondly. "Dick was a good provider. We loved one another, and we were determined to be successful in raising a family."

Known as "Captain Midnight" because he liked the late shifts, Dick piloted ferries. Betty, a people person, never had to look for a job because employers recruited her. Over the years, she worked at the Burton Mercantile, the drug store, the post office, and K2. She sang in the Methodist Church choir, served as Senior Center Board president, and coached girls' softball. She knitted, crocheted, and did watercolor painting. She and Dick sailed a sloop around Puget Sound and, when they retired, explored the country in a travel trailer.

She chuckles, remembering a couple of sailing trips with five women neighbors. She really wasn't much of a sailor and would have preferred a power boat. But Dick said go ahead. "We were out several days, and he never called or anything," she laughs.

We loved one another and determined to be successful in raising a family.

ENJOY YOUR WORK
Dick Franklin

When he and his wife moved from Los Angeles to retirement on Vashon four decades ago, there was no way Dick Franklin, a thoughtful, purposeful fellow, "was going to sit and vegetate." After a high-powered career as a human resources and business manager at electronics, aerospace, and safety equipment firms, Dick wanted to do something on Vashon. He bought a small real estate company that came with a state licensing franchise. He sold the real estate business but kept the licensing office under the lofty corporate title of International Development Services.

And there, squeezed between an alley, a former barbershop, and the back of Herban Bloom, Dick manages the sale and renewal of vehicle, hunting, and fishing licenses. His compact office space has a long counter, a desk, a wall of notices, a pail for a leak in the ceiling, and a prominent sign: Cash or Check Only. He has one employee. Hours are 1-4pm, Tuesday-Saturday.

It's a far cry from his earlier life. Yet Dick, an avid fisherman and ex-Vashon fire commissioner, enjoys it as much as the heady years of being a corporate hotshot.

The older of two boys born to an auto mechanic and a homemaker, he grew up in Spokane, where he excelled in math and science at Rogers High School. At 17, he enlisted in the Navy just as World War II was ending. The Navy kept him, active and in the Reserve, at naval air stations in California through the Korean War. The GI Bill helped him earn a BA in industrial psychology at WSU and an MA at UCLA. He married, built a home in an LA suburb, and raised four kids.

A job with the LA School District managing a student work experience program led to HR management positions with a succession of companies. In the late 1950s, Dick overcame staff resistance to hire the first Black man at a 500-employee electronics firm. As director of industrial relations for a safety equipment corporation, he traveled the country negotiating local contracts with machinist, auto, teamster, and textile worker unions. "It was stressful," he says, "but I enjoyed the give and take in effecting a contract that was fair to the company and to its employees." And, he admits a bit sheepishly, "I was good at it."

Dick Franklin caught this 4-foot, 70-pound halibut on a rod and reel.

EVERY DAY IS A REAL PRIZE
Rich Nelson

Rich Nelson, who spent 13 years in the Navy Reserve and then another 17 years in the Army National Guard, took on some rather unusual military assignments. He taught military science in France. He went underground with South Korean troops to eavesdrop on North Korea. And, he worked undercover, in civilian clothes, with the code name "Batman." His assignment: Infiltrate suspect National Guard units to finger drug traffickers and identify incompetent officers.

"One time we got a request from the mayor of Port Angeles to help investigate drug trafficking," recalls Rich, a dapper fellow with a neatly trimmed mustache. Sleuthing, however, was something Rich did on the side over a long career teaching biology at middle and high schools in Tacoma. At Wilson High School, he wore a white lab coat and was nicknamed "Mr. Science."

The middle child of a Swedish immigrant and a Norwegian-American homemaker, Rich moved from a Montana ranch to Tacoma when his dad got a job with the

12-year-old Rich Nelson, in a white gown pinned with a white carnation, at his confirmation at Luther Memorial Lutheran Church in Tacoma in 1943.

Northern Pacific. He graduated from Lincoln High School, where he was a self-described "mediocre athlete" on the school's 1949 state championship football team. At 17, he signed up for the Navy Reserve and was trained to be a submariner.

"I was a real screwup," Rich admits, "a playboy." He taught skiing at Snoqualmie Pass, Crystal Mountain, and even Davos, Switzerland. He met lots of girls. In 1950, he wed one of them, Carole Preuss, a cheerleader who gave him two children and 52 years of happy marriage. When she died of cancer in 2001, Rich was lost. He wandered around the Northwest, returned to the Montana ranch, and finally flew off to Norway to grieve with relatives.

The following year he met Harriet Shull on Valentine's Day. They were married in Norway three months later and set up life together on Vashon. "I'm a lucky guy," Rich says, "and I take every day as a real prize."

EXPECT THE UNEXPECTED
Bill Bryce

One might think that with a degree in aeronautical engineering from the University of Toronto followed by a two-year fellowship at a UK aeronautics college, Bill Bryce was set for life. Not so. Bill, whose expertise was aeroelasticity, found jobs. But the jobs went belly-up when the planes did. On a Friday afternoon in 1959, the public address system announced that he and 14,000 other employees were done because the prime minister had just canceled the Avro Arrow, an interceptor aircraft hailed as Canada's "greatest plane that never was."

Born and raised in Ottawa, Bill left Canada for the US once he had a security clearance to work at North American Aviation in Columbus, Ohio. That led to a job in Seattle on Boeing's supersonic transport jets. "What a disaster that was," Bill says of the aborted SST. He received a 10-year pin and a layoff notice the same week. After brief jobs on the Saturn rocket in New Orleans and on hovercrafts in Tacoma, Boeing called Bill back to help modify the 747 carrying the space shuttle. Next it was the E-6, a militarized 707 designed to communicate with submarines by dipping an antenna into the sea. The plane had its challenges. Bill chuckles, recalling test flights in which excessive rudder vibration blew off vertical tail sections over Boeing Field.

In 1995, Bill took a Boeing buyout that gave him more time on Vashon, where he, his wife, Dolores, and their four children had lived since 1967. He took up bridge and upped his daily walks from two miles to 12. Virtually every day you could see Bill, his gait tilted left from nerve damage, striding down the main highway, indifferent to the weather. By the time age and neuropathy ended his daily walk, Bill had logged 55,000 miles. His world shrank more when Dolores died last October.

Bill Bryce helped modify the Boeing 747 to carry the space shuttle.

EXPERIENCE THE ARTS
Pam McMahan

In a tiny garden next to the Vashon Pharmacy is a shiny, saucer-shaped steel sculpture that makes music thanks to a program that Pam McMahan helped begin 35 years ago. Island artist Ela Lamblin and a crew of Vashon High School physics students designed and built the imaginative work through the Vashon Artists in Schools program. Every year the program pairs local artists with teachers to create some 15 to 20 immersive art experiences with students.

Pam, while not an artist herself, is convinced that the visual arts, music, theater, and dance are absolutely essential on "the journey of life." "Art deals with ambiguity," she says. "It finds meaning in abstraction." Her two daughters, products of Vashon schools, got the message. One is a professor of comparative literature and film studies; the other, a professional violist.

The second of four children born to an insurance adjuster and a homemaker, Pam grew up in what was then rural Bellevue and walked two miles of muddy road to school. While the nuns at Sacred Heart School and Holy Names Academy provided Pam with a rigorous education ("compulsory arbitration in labor management disputes" was a high school debate topic), she began the University of Washington feeling "overwhelmed," unsure of herself.

It was 1967. "And here I had no idea it was the Summer of Love," she says. Eventually Pam majored in English, minored in political science, protested against the Vietnam War, and found a research job with the Association of Washington Cities in Olympia. The job made her an expert on legal and legislative issues related to towns and cities. She prepared testimony for lobbyists, wrote the association's newsletter, and learned the art of finding grant money, a skill she employed masterfully in sustaining the Artists in Schools program.

In 1974, she married Jake Schlumpf, a commercial fisherman soon to be a science teacher, and the couple moved to Vashon. For 20 years, they lived on the island and raised their daughters. In 1996, Jake's career shift from classroom teaching to educational technology took them first to Houston, then Philadelphia, Seattle, and Cambridge, Massachusetts. In 2012, they returned to Vashon, where Pam resumed where she had left off. She became the coordinator for Vashon Artists in Schools.

Savvy Rodriguez, 7, laughs at the whimsical sculpture created through a school arts program coordinated by Pam McMahan.

EXPERIENCE THE WORLD
Elise Lindgren

There's no obvious connection between surviving gale-force winds and 30-foot seas in a sailboat in the North Pacific and treating displaced Ugandans in the midst of an Ebola outbreak, but Elise Lindgren makes one. It's about getting out of yourself and experiencing the world.

In 1992 Elise, an RN and nursing teacher, and her husband, Cliff, a construction manager, quit their jobs, bought a 35-foot sailboat (the "Illusion"), and with their 10-year-old son set off on a two-year sailing adventure from Vashon to New Zealand. They were only a few days out when a huge storm hit. They took down the sails and put out 200 feet of anchor chain off the stern. But still the gale was so furious they feared it would pitchpole the boat. It was the most harrowing experience of the voyage. "It taught us," Elise says, "that we weren't going to fall apart."

It taught us that we weren't going to fall apart.

That made it easier for Elise to take short leaves from teaching at Highline College to volunteer for disaster nursing with Northwest Medical Teams. She did two stints in Uganda treating war-traumatized villagers and another caring for earthquake survivors in Haiti. "I learned very quickly about malaria and malnutrition," she says.

Born and raised in Minneapolis, the daughter of a vocational tech teacher and a secretary, Elise was 18 when she met Cliff, a college guy, at Al's Breakfast Cafe, where she was the omelette chef. They've been together ever since. In 1976, they came west to visit a friend and discovered Vashon. They stayed, bought a home, and started a family. Elise waitressed, finished a nursing program at Tacoma Community College, worked at Tacoma General, and later earned a Master's in community health nursing at the University of Washington. With help from Providence, she started a hospice program on the island.

Although Elise no longer sails, her family does. Her son, daughter-in-law, and two granddaughters sold their Vashon home, bought a sailboat, and are bound for New Zealand in August.

FAITH IS 'HANDS ON'
Bev Skeffington

Bev Skeffington, who operates Vashon's only full-service travel agency, is a "hands-on" kind of person. She deals with clients person-to-person. She books tickets, offers guidance, and provides advice unlikely to be found on Google. For instance: Avoid New York's JFK Airport; the lines are long, and the TSA agents are rude.

A get 'er done gal, Bev started out to be a teacher. Born and raised on Long Island, New York, she was the second child of a grade school principal and a homemaker. She dutifully followed her sister to Moravian College in Pennsylvania, where she completed an education degree.

But after student teaching, she'd had enough and joined VISTA, which sent her to St. Luke's Hospital in Manhattan as a social work aide. Bev fell in love with the Big Apple. When her VISTA term was up, she waitressed on the upper West Side until a "disastrous romantic relationship" sent her back home to mom and dad. One day she saw an ad for flight attendants with a charter airline that flew troops and their families all over the globe. She got the job and began a new romance—with travel.

Bev Skeffington and two fellow Habitat for Humanity volunteers at work on a two-house building project in King County.

A post-college reunion in Pennsylvania, however, changed the trajectory of Bev's life. She got reacquainted with Jacq Skeffington, a fellow alumnus. They fell in love. After the Coast Guard sent Jacq to Seattle, Bev followed. They settled on Vashon, where, in 1979, they quietly married in the Presbyterian Church. Jacq was Catholic and Bev was Protestant, so neither told their parents. Forty years and two children later, they're still married and committed to the church.

On Vashon, Bev waitressed at the Spinnaker, substitute-taught in schools, built homes for Habitat for Humanity, began her travel agency, sat the night with hospice patients, and, at Vashon Presbyterian, directed and sang in the choir, played the harp, and served as an elder and a deacon. "Faith," she says, "keeps you centered."

FEED HUNGRY KIDS
Nancy Radford

Every school weekend some 30 Vashon kids go home with a bag of food that will get them through two breakfasts, two lunches, two dinners, and snacks because Nancy Radford had an idea that wouldn't let go. Through determined organization, she figured Vashon could help financially strapped families feed their children on weekends when schools don't provide lunches (22 percent of Vashon's school kids qualify for free or low-cost lunches). Thus was born Backpack Pantry.

Nancy won over the school district, which identifies the children most in need. Every week those children quietly receive a bag of non-perishable food for their backpacks. It typically contains noodles, oatmeal, fruit, canned tuna, chicken or spaghetti along with crackers, granola bars, and pudding. The food, valued at $7 a bag, is donated or purchased at reduced cost. Nancy, who ran for unofficial mayor of Vashon last year to raise money for Backpack Pantry, heads the food-soliciting, fundraising, packaging, and delivery operation.

A grandmother of eight, she says, "There's no sense in trying to teach kids if they haven't eaten."

One of five children, Nancy grew up in Ballard and graduated from Holy Angels High School. She later met Dick Radford, a Boeing finance officer. The couple married in 1963, had five children in seven years, and moved from Seattle to Vashon in 1971. They bought Dick's parents' house on Maury Island, where Nancy still lives today. Dick passed away in 1993.

While child-raising, Nancy completed night courses in education at three universities. For 13 years she worked in Vashon schools as a special education aide. Then she switched to helping vulnerable adults, eventually becoming director of a Bremerton-based nonprofit agency that trained and found employment for the developmentally disabled. She retired in 1990 but has been plenty busy ever since.

There's no sense in trying to teach kids if they haven't eaten.

FIGURE IT OUT
Keith Prior

A jovial fellow who delights in witticisms, Keith Prior has spent his life figuring things out. Today he is the volunteer "data generalist" for the Senior Center's Vashon Villages project, an effort to create neighborly communities of seniors that better meet their needs.

Keith's latest assignment follows a long career in county, state, and contract jobs in which he collected and analyzed data and then proposed ways to make things better. He helped improve anti-poverty, health care, and economic opportunity programs in Kern and Shasta Counties in California. He conducted a child care study for the administration of Gov. Jerry Brown. For the National Institute of Mental Health, he did research in 40 of the state's 58 counties to answer questions on how to de-institutionalize mental patients from hospitals to community care. And for 25 years, he was an analyst at UC Davis, answering questions on issues in K-12 and higher education. After retirement, the university asked him back to manage an environmental impact study on restoring 15,000 acres of wetlands.

"I'm a dilettante," Keith chuckles. "Architecture, sociology, political psychology — you name it." In fact, a chance encounter hitchhiking introduced him to Saul Alinksy, the renowned community organizer, and a $250-per-month stipend organizing with Cesar Chavez and the United Farm Workers.

Born in Hollywood the middle child of three, Keith grew up in Montrose, California in a privileged family with "an overdeveloped sense of entitlement." Through his father's job as manager of an oil company owned by movie stars, he met Red Skelton, John Wayne, and the Cisco Kid. The family later moved to Bakersfield, where Keith's high school graduation class numbered 1,100. He did two years of community college and enrolled at the University of Washington, planning to be a naval architect until the hitchhiking encounter put him on a new path.

Keith Prior, new director of the Shasta County Anti-Poverty Agency, and deputy director Lee Macy in 1972.

Seventy years after those first idyllic summers staying with his maternal grandmother in Burton, Keith convinced his wife, Karen Bray, to move to Vashon. They found a home in Gold Beach, where Keith, still the would-be naval architect, is building several boats.

FIND BALANCE
Donna Caulton

Donna Caulton, an artist who paints in bright, bold acrylics, calls herself a "gypsy" because she's dwelt in such divergent places. She's lived on a naval air base in Nevada, an art studio loft in Pioneer Square, a solar-powered Airstream trailer off the grid in Eastern Washington, and an adobe house in the mountains of New Mexico. Nowadays, she paints in a light-bathed studio behind her daughter's house on Vashon.

Her abstract and repeated imagery focuses on the symbiotic relationship of plants, animals, the sun, and the moon. "My paintings are tales of balance in the natural world, the world as it should be," Donna says.

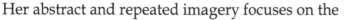

Southwest Indian art was a curious pursuit for a New Jersey girl who grew up in a family of six that she describes as "bereft of creative expression." Dad installed propane pumps and mom was a homemaker. Both imposed "extreme restrictions." A quiet, timid, serious student, Donna fled outdoors, reveling in the beauty of nearby forests and farms. Friends called her "nature girl."

Her senior year of high school, the family moved to Columbia, South Carolina, which Donna recalls as hot, conformist, and unfond of Yankees. She completed a hospital nursing program, where she met a lab tech bound for medical school and married him within three months. They had two kids in 16 months. He finished his MD and joined the Navy, which sent the family to Nevada. With his discharge, they settled in Redmond, Oregon, where one day he decided the marriage was over. "I was demolished," Donna says, "yet I began to find my own pathway."

She began traveling. Her exploration of Hopi ruins in the Southwest and Inca temples in Peru nourished Donna's emerging love of art. With part-time nursing paying the bills, she completed an art degree at Evergreen State, opened her studio in Seattle, and began painting first in the Northwest, then in New Mexico. She taught watercolor as artist-in-residence at Washington state prisons and collaborated with four New Mexico women artists in painting creation-migration stories. Her work won awards and was exhibited at galleries and museums (see DonnaCaulton.com).

"Sacred Ground" by Donna Caulton, whose art is influenced by both the Southwest and the Northwest.

For Donna, painting created an equilibrium, a balance in life and in a world that so needs it.

FIND THE RIGHT PARTNER
June Dinsmore

Divide the life of June Dinsmore in two: Before Tom and After Tom. Before Tom, June was caught in a miserable marriage, cut off from others. Quiet and self-sacrificing, she stuck it out for 23 years until her younger son was an adult. "My son didn't leave home when he turned 21," she says. "His mother did."

At age 40, single and unencumbered, June "did things I should have done at 18." She partied; she made friends. And on a Fourth of July weekend, she went out on a hastily arranged double date with a Vashon guy who took the foursome on a sailing cruise in his trimaran. "Tom and I started talking," says June, "and we haven't stopped since." After a year of courting on weekends, they married.

June grew up in north Seattle, the older of two children born to a homemaker mom and a father who owned a light bulb business and read the Sunday comics to his kids. Home was happy enough, but school life unraveled when the family moved to the Ravenna neighborhood. June started Roosevelt High School knowing no one. An average student, she graduated and, at 17, wed an older man. Over the next two decades, she raised their two boys and worked as a secretary for the Bellevue School District.

June Dinsmore, here in formal attire, was the first woman elected "Commodore" of the Quartermaster Yacht Club.

Then came Tom. The newlyweds first lived in a house that Tom had barged years earlier to Burton and, when it burned to the ground, bought a view home on the north end. June became a Vashon Schools secretary, doubling as informal nurse and problem-solver, and later took a position as an administrative assistant in King County Superior Court. Meanwhile, Tom introduced her to sailing. With June at the helm, they explored the far reaches of Puget Sound. At the Quartermaster Yacht Club, June became the first woman to be elected "Commodore," the club's presiding officer.

On Vashon, June has had a social life that would have been unimaginable to her 40 years ago. Aside from sailing, she's involved with the Garden Club, the Women's Club, and Granny's Attic. What happened? "Tom," she says. "He made all the difference."

FIND YOUR CALLING
Tom Craighead

Tom Craighead walked out into the chill night air on a remote island in Maine and knew he was staring into the abyss. He was angry, aimless, drinking too much and, at 25, desperate. He had quit the University of Montana just two incomplete papers short of graduation. He had once planned to go to the US Naval Academy and, like his father, serve the country. But the Vietnam War, his resistance to authority, and a week of convalescing at the Bethesda Naval Hospital turned his head around. Tom was a civilian recovering from knee surgery. The young Marines in his open ward were recovering from war. He watched as the man next to him died.

On that frigid Maine night, Tom looked up and said, "Lord, I guess you're out there, take me." A half-century later, he calls it "the key anchoring point in my life." God, he decided, had plans for him.

But God was slow to show the way. Tom, a quiet, calm, contemplative sort, resumed going to church. He then apprenticed himself to an Episcopal bishop in Maryland, where he ran parish youth groups and Bible studies. He thought he heard a faint call to priesthood. Conflicted, he took seven on-and-off years to complete Episcopal seminary in New York City and be ordained.

His first priest job was at stately St. Paul's Cathedral in Buffalo, where he met and married Lornie Walker, a fallen-away Episcopalian. They had two sons as Tom completed three years in Buffalo and then six more as a vicar in Burlington, Vermont. Spiritual care was great but church administration bored him. Tom took a sabbatical to complete an MSW in family counseling, and the family headed to Seattle. He did mental health and family therapy and returned to parish ministry in Port Orchard. Still, this wasn't it.

At age 50 he found a job as a hospice chaplain with CHI Franciscan in Tacoma. Suddenly he was in homes and hospitals with folks who realized this conversation might be their last. Many wanted to go deep, talk heart-to-heart, and try to forgive themselves. Tom was there to help them let go. This, he knew, was his true calling.

It was the key anchoring point in my life.

FIND YOUR LOVE
Raynor Christianson

When his wife of 40 years died of brain cancer, Raynor Christianson fell into a deep, black hole. "Bereavement was overwhelming," he recalls.

He had met Nicole, an attractive, vivacious blonde, when they were both teenagers growing up in greater Los Angeles. They married when she was 19 and he was 23. Their wanderlust took them everywhere. For a while, they lived on a 40-foot ketch in Marina del Rey. They sailed the boat through hurricane winds, got to the Bay Area, and traded the boat for a cabin in the Redwoods. Next they decided to try suburbia. First it was Sunnyvale and then later, with two kids in hand, it was Portland and finally Kirkland.

We never settled down; we just liked change.

"We never settled down," Raynor says. "It wasn't because of jobs; we just liked change."

When Nicole passed away in 2005, Raynor was working as a software tester at Microsoft. The job was the last in a technical career that spanned 48 years, beginning with electrical accounting machines in Santa Monica, which morphed into computer programming in Sunnyvale, then leaped from test engineering to network analyzing in Portland and Redmond. The tech companies where he worked expanded, contracted, and sometimes disappeared. It was an exhilarating and excruciating experience.

But not nearly as difficult as his wife's slow death. One day his condo neighbors persuaded him to take a bridge class. He loved the game so much that he began playing several times a week. He wasn't fussy about partners. He played with anyone.

In 2007, he met Mary Van Gemert, and a year later the two decided to live together in her Burton home. Raynor's arrival was a big boost for the Vashon Bridge Club. He is a tireless advocate for the game, recruiting players wherever he finds them. After all, bridge had restored him.

FIX IT
Michael O'Donnell

Michael O'Donnell credits seniors for his thriving on-island computer consulting business, Sound Computing. A life-long computer hobbyist, he saw an item in the *Beachcomber* about the Vashon Computer Club and decided to attend. Seniors were there in abundance with all sorts of technical questions: How do I transmit a photo? How do I set up a printer? How do I access the internet on my cell phone?

Michael, who once subscribed to eight computer magazines, answered their questions and realized here was a business opportunity. He could make a living fixing software problems and repairing computers in people's homes and businesses. So, he did, becoming Vashon's go-to computer repairman entirely by word of mouth. He loves it. "I get to meet the most amazing people, see some fantastic artwork, and hear the most wonderful stories," says Michael, a warm, open, likable guy who gets around COVID by controlling computers remotely.

The middle child of a Kidney Foundation executive and a homemaker, Michael grew up in Ypsilanti, Michigan. When he was five, his father died in an auto accident. His mother's subsequent two marriages didn't last, and school was tough. He didn't apply himself, didn't fit in, and got bullied. Senior year he dropped out. "I just stopped showing up," he recalls, "and nobody noticed."

At 17, he was working as a bartender's assistant in a night club. By 20, he was the night club's manager, directing a staff of 30. And, at 24, he started running corporate dinner houses, first in Michigan and then in Houston. He realized he had a talent that employers prized: He could identify problems and solve them. In Texas, Michael met and married a successful pharmaceutical consultant who needed help using tech to manage her business. He said he'd do it, abandoned the restaurant biz, and eventually moved with her to Vashon, which, he says, they found by accident.

The marriage ended in 2010. Five years ago, Michael was the volunteer bartender at an island art auction when he met Carrie Sikorski. A matchmaker friend fanned the spark that soon flamed between them, and they've been together ever since.

I get to meet the most amazing people, see some fantastic artwork, and hear the most wonderful stories.

GET THE FACTS
Jay Becker

Jay Becker, a newspaperman since high school, follows the old reporter's adage: "If your mother says she loves you, check it out." He says he's dismayed that so many folks are suckered by "fake news."

A short, bearded man who carries a notepad in his hip pocket, Jay lists the signs of what he calls "malarkey": A story that has no attribution or questionable sources, is based on hearsay, or offers no evidence of what it is alleging. "Be a skeptic," he says. "Question anything somebody thinks is news. Analyze, verify, and corroborate."

Question anything somebody thinks is news. Analyze, verify, and corroborate.

Born in Seattle, Jay had an itinerant childhood as his dad moved about the state working as a phone company manager, a grocer, an oyster farmer, and a Boeing engineer. Eventually the family settled in Olympia, where Jay took photos for the high school yearbook. He got hooked on journalism. He won a "table waiting" scholarship to Stanford, where he met Joan, now his wife of 63 years, and found his first paid news job at a weekly in Marin County.

When the Army drafted him in 1955, he wheedled a position with the public information office at Fort Riley, Kansas, where he and Joan had the first of their three boys. After the Army, the young family returned to Washington, where Jay worked for newspapers in Ellensburg, Poulsbo, and Kirkland. A chance encounter at a GOP county convention got him a job establishing a tabloid newspaper for the Seattle Chamber of Commerce. He later worked as a community relations manager for Weyerhaeuser. But he and Joan hankered for their own newspaper and life on an island.

In 1975 "we hocked our house in Kirkland to make a down payment on the *Beachcomber* and moved to Vashon," Jay says. The hours were so long that Jay sometimes slept on the office floor. But they made a go of it, running the paper until they retired in 1995.

GIVE ME A CHANCE
Jim Brown

It was a drug deal that brought Jim Brown to Vashon in 1993. A self-described "full-blown alcoholic," he was selling pot and cocaine and drinking himself senseless. His life was a train wreck.

His parents, a comptroller and a homemaker, moved him and his two younger sisters from New Jersey to Jackson, Mississippi when Jim was 16. He had dropped out of school, detested the South ("ignorant, backward, prejudiced people"), and hated his dad. So he left, hitchhiking to Los Angeles, where he loaded trucks by day and slept in them at night. At 17, he enlisted in the Army ("a big mistake since I couldn't take orders"), was sent to Vietnam, and went AWOL on a stopover back to the States. In Mississippi, he fell for a girl and followed her to Austin. She went to college; he got into drugs—bigtime.

From there, Jim pursued an itinerant life of boozing, doping, and ruined relationships. He married a Mississippi woman but couldn't deal with her two kids. He married a Michigan woman with three boys and a baseball bat that she tried to bring down on his head. He hit her and walked out. He married a third time in Seattle, took his bride to Alaska, and "lied to her badly." "I couldn't be trusted," he candidly admits. "I wasn't worth a damn."

Along the way, Jim cooked, tended bar, did construction, drove trucks, and worked on an oil survey crew. But mostly he drank, got high, and played pool for money. He fancied college towns, renting rooms in Austin, Ann Arbor, Eugene, and Seattle. His reprehensible treatment of his third wife convinced him to enter alcoholism treatment. He stayed sober for several years but when he moved to Vashon, he was drinking and shooting coke again.

> ## *People on Vashon gave me a chance to believe in myself.*

"Vashon saved me," Jim says, "because Pete Chorak and Jimmy Matsumoto gave me a chance." Chorak, a tavern owner, paid Jim to clean up after closing and let him sleep on the premises. Matsumoto, a contractor, gave him a chainsaw and permission to sell firewood from cleared property. Eventually, Jim checked back into alcoholism treatment, got sober, and ran Matsumoto's construction company. "I haven't had a drink in 25 years," Jim says. "People on Vashon gave me a chance to believe in myself."

GO FOR IT
Susan Rogers

Susan Rogers didn't start out to be adventurous. The only child of an International Paper salesman and a homemaker, she grew up in a little pink house in the planned community of Levittown, Pennsylvania. She graduated from a small, all-girls Catholic high school and, despite her mother's urging that she travel first, Susan quickly enrolled in nearby St. Francis College.

While at St. Francis, she happened to visit a friend at Penn State. And wow, were her eyes opened! "I saw a bigger world out there," Susan recalls. She transferred to Penn State, pledged Tri-Delta Sorority, earned a degree in elementary education, and married a guy her parents rejected.

The guy took her to Hawaii, where she taught fourth grade, completed an M.Ed in communications, and landed a state job producing guidance and health television programs for kids. She loved it, but she and her hubby got the travel bug and went off to Mexico and Guatemala. They camped on the beach, scuba dived, and immersed themselves in local culture. "Latin America shifted my consciousness," Susan says.

Susan Rogers, production supervisor of a Hawaii public TV health program for kids, joins the director and a student on the set in 1971.

So much so that she traded her husband for San Francisco, where she embraced Eastern spirituality. "I was looking for love," Susan explains, "but then I realized it was already inside me." She became a disciple of the Maharaji, an Indian guru, and relocated to the movement's headquarters in Denver, where she met Richard, another disciple. Ever adventurous, they married by a waterfall in Jamaica and settled in Miami, where Susan did a dizzying number of jobs including clerk in a Jewish grocery, editorial assistant at a diving magazine, administrative representative at Mt. Sinai Medical Center, and personal assistant to Philip Michael Thomas, co-star of *Miami Vice*.

After she and Richard moved to Vashon in 1989, Susan sought work closer to her spiritual core. She was an instructor and registrar at Centerpoint Institute for Life and Career Renewal in Seattle, did elder care on the Island, and worked as Dr. Elmer Carlson's chiropractic assistant. "If something attracts me, I go for it," she says.

GO FOR WHAT YOU WANT
Annie Strandberg

Annie Strandberg was a 16-year-old junior at Olympia High School when she had second thoughts about Lars, the Finnish immigrant who had invited her to a high school wrestling match. She had declined. "Then I thought—hmmm," she recalls. "The tolo dance is coming up." But in order to ask Lars, she had to persuade her girlfriend to invite Phil, the guy she had been dating. She made that happen and Lars was hers. He's been hers ever since.

Born Annie VanDyke, the youngest of four girls in a Catholic family of five children, she grew up in Olympia. Her father ran a gas station. Her mother was an RN. After high school, Annie started college at Seattle University but soon found that she preferred the hands-on nursing program at nearby Cabrini Hospital. She earned a nursing diploma and began a career that took her to several area hospitals. Annie loved caring for people at their most personal and vulnerable moments. "It is so rewarding," she says.

She also worked for Lars, whom she married in 1970. She helped manage his pharmaceutical business, including giving flu shots to thousands of patients, a task that wasn't easy with two young daughters at home.

While nursing was Annie's day job, her other passion has been music. She began piano at age eight, learned the ukulele at 12, and played and sang folk music at coffee houses and festivals—including Folklife—during and after college. After she

and Lars moved to Vashon in 1989, she sang with the island's first community choir and was involved with Drama Dock and Vashon High School musical theater productions. A soprano, she now sings with the island's Free Range Choir.

In retirement, Annie and Lars live in the Gold Beach house that, to the dismay of some neighbors, they had barged to the island as a summer shack three decades ago. It's been much improved, enlarged, and surrounded with gardens. There's a piano and Annie sings.

Annie Strandberg and her dog, Lexie, on the driftwood-strewn shore near her home at Gold Beach.

GO TO THE WOODS
Sean Malone

Sean Malone, a woodcutter, filmmaker, ham
radio operator, and columnist for *The Loop*, lives
in a hobbit-like log cabin on a steep slope above
Magnolia Beach. He heats entirely with wood. Two
cords a year. His socks dry on the wood beams
above the fireplace. The one-room cabin, built in
1955, was red-tagged for slides when Sean bought it
for a song 15 years ago and repaired it.

In returning to Vashon from the small Eastern
Washington logging town of Republic, Sean had
gone full circle. The oldest of four children born to a painting contractor and a
homemaker, he grew up on the island in the 1950s. He graduated from Seattle Prep,
where he won an elocution contest with his rendition of "Swan Lake Ballet by Andy
Griffith." He briefly went to Seattle University, dropped out to become a "ski bum,"
then got drafted into the Army and sent to Korea.

"That experience convinced me to return to SU," says Sean, a plain-spoken guy
who wears plaid wool shirts, suspendered jeans, and work boots. "I doubled
my grade point." He earned a BA in journalism, married an SU girl, had two
children and a job producing short documentaries for KING-TV. He directed films
about an old fisherman who'd lost his boat in a storm, about distillery workers
producing Seagram's whiskey in a 16th-century castle in Scotland, and about young
professionals who went hippie and were living on the mud flats outside Maplewood,
British Columbia.

But when KING closed its film operation, things went south. Sean's independent film
efforts failed. So did his marriage. In 1982, dejected and jobless, he abandoned the
bright lights of Seattle and "went to the woods."

He moved to Republic, where he cut firewood, set up a still, and moonlighted as a
night watchman at a gold mine. He figures he cut 3,000 cords in his 22 years there.
Now he's cutting wood again on Vashon.

Sean Malone cuts a downed alder tree off power lines on Vashon's Pillsbury Road.

GOD HAS SERVED ME WELL
Marilyn Klob

Marilyn Klob grew up an only child in a happy home centered on faith and church life in Hamilton, Ohio. She walked two blocks to grade school at St. Peter in Chains and came home for lunch. She graduated from all-girls Notre Dame High School and went off to Indianapolis to earn an education degree at Marian College, another all-girls school. Her first post-college job was as a social worker placing foster kids for Catholic Charities. Later she taught second grade at St. Stephen School back home in Hamilton.

I've always wanted to be helping someone.

Decades later, Marilyn is active at St. John Vianney Church on Vashon. "I've always wanted to be helping someone," says Marilyn, an attentive, bright-eyed grandma who just celebrated her 90th birthday. "God has helped me by putting the right people in my life."

God's plans for Marilyn were not her parents' plans. Her father, an opera-loving accountant whose daughter was blessed with a lyric soprano voice, thought she would be an opera star. Her mother, a self-taught pianist with perfect pitch, figured Marilyn for a career in music and theater. Marilyn had started playing piano in second grade and began voice lessons at 13. By college, she was doing summer stock theater in Vermont. She studied a year at the prestigious Cincinnati Conservatory of Music and, at Marian College, was mentored by a nationally recognized voice specialist.

But when Marilyn and her college roommate headed off to New York City to audition for the big time, it was a bust. They stood in line after line to audition for Broadway shows but got nowhere. A month later, Marilyn was back in Hamilton and soon helping foster kids in Cincinnati.

She married her high school sweetheart John Klob, who shortened his name from "Kloboucnik," and nine years later their only child, a daughter, arrived. John's accounting job with General Foods took them from Ohio to California, Colorado, and New England. With his retirement in 2004, they moved to Vashon to be near their daughter's family. John died in 2017 but Marilyn shoulders on, comforted by memories, family, friends, and faith.

GOD PROVIDES
Jack Watney

A modest, patient, and thoughtful retiree, Jack Watney realizes that—but for the grace of God—his life could have taken some wrong turns. "The Lord has been very gentle with me," he says.

The older of two boys raised by an aeronautical engineer and a schoolteacher on the hill above Seattle's Boeing Plant 2, Jack embraced the Depression-era values of his parents: thrift, discipline, responsibility, thankfulness. But after the family moved to Three Tree Point in Burien, he befriended a mischievous middle schooler. The two boys' unsupervised escapades included rowing to Vashon without life vests, an unexpected blast from a .38 revolver, and bedeviling boats barreling down the Sound. And music, lots of music. By the time Jack graduated from Highline High School, he was making money playing trombone in a big band, "The 99ers."

Nonetheless, he dutifully started engineering school at the UW, only to drop out and be drafted. The Army sent him to Fort Eustis, Virginia, to play trombone in the band. In the midst of the civil rights era, enlisted life in the deep South was an unnerving culture shock. God intervened. And Jack emerged from the Army as "a repurposed individual," knowing he would be an engineer.

He returned to Seattle, earned BS and MS degrees in mechanical engineering at the UW, and went to work at Boeing. He met Nancy, a nurse and now his wife of 54 years, in the laundry room of an Eastlake apartment building. The couple bought their first and only home in Burton in 1972 and raised two kids.

Jack worked his whole career at Boeing, with the exception of a year and a half at McDonnell Douglas in St. Louis during the Boeing bust of the late '60s. He and Nancy still have their correspondence from the time they were apart. Eventually Boeing rehired Jack to apply his engineering skills to programs such as the Air Force's cruise missile and a satellite that orbited Venus and Mercury. Overall, life's been good, he says, "because God's in control."

The Lord has been very gentle with me.

HEED THE VULNERABLE
Julia Lakey

A theme that runs through the life of Julia Lakey is a concern for the vulnerable. She has worked with the deaf, with refugees, and with at-risk kids. In recent years, she has focused on the vulnerability of flora, fauna, and nature in general.

An optimist with can-do solutions, Julia grew up an adopted child who remained connected to her chaotic biological family. "I'm an only child and one of 12," she says. Home was seven acres of rattlesnake wilderness alongside sandstone mountains outside Chatsworth, California. She blew a toy trumpet down tarantula holes to rouse the giant spiders, including her favorite, Neal. Dad was an advertising salesman at the Van Nuys News; mom ran the ranch.

A diligent student, Julia skipped second grade and graduated as high school salutatorian at 16. She married her high school sweetheart. After both graduated from Cal Lutheran, they earned master's degrees in educating the deaf and taught at the Kansas State School for the Deaf. But they missed the West. In the summer of 1976, they discovered Vashon and never looked back.

Julia found two part-time jobs, teaching the deaf at Seattle Central Community College and English to refugees at Renton Technical College. The refugees spoke 26 different languages, a hurdle she leaped by developing an immigrant-friendly approach to English. Her curriculum grew into a book and a job with the Center for

Vashon is committed to providing a "sustainable wildlife habitat" thanks to a drive led by Julia Lakey.

Applied Linguistics that took her to refugee camps in Asia and resettlement communities in the US. With the birth of her daughter, however, Julia exchanged the travel for Gig Harbor High School, where she taught special ed, English, and humanities.

A second marriage, to island musician Steve Self in 1991, came with three additional daughters and, after her retirement from teaching in 1994, led Julia into house painting, gardening, and landscaping. Increasingly, she focused on her island environment. She co-founded Zero Waste Vashon. She led the drive to certify Vashon as a wildlife habitat community. And, most recently, she set up the Pollinator Project, a demonstration garden of native wildflowers at Matsuda Farm to attract birds and bees. "Let's give voice," she says, "to the little things that run the world."

HELP OTHERS
George Eustice

In 1996, after he nearly burned to death in a freak accident, George Eustice decided to become Santa Claus.

"I was not going to give up," George recalled. Burned over half of his body, he spent 12 weeks in the Harborview burn unit, had 14 skin-grafting operations and endured months of daily physical therapy.

Yet George became the island's Santa Claus. Blessed with a big beard, an ample belly, and a booming voice, he is friendly and welcoming. "How you doing, boss?" is his standard greeting. The recorded message on his home phone says, "Sorry I'm not here. I must be out feeding the reindeer."

Born into a blue-collar family in West Seattle, George cannot remember a time when he didn't work. He labored as a box boy, a caddy, a janitor, and a bakery supply driver. He met Sandy, now his wife of nearly 50 years, when he and his best buddy switched dates after the Holy Rosary High School prom. The two lovers, just 18, eloped to Coeur d'Alene three months later, phoning their parents after the wedding vows were pronounced.

George and Sandy soon had two children— 14 months apart—and moved to Vashon in 1966. Sandy worked as a school librarian, and George drove a delivery truck all over Washington and Oregon. He served as a volunteer firefighter, a Jaycee, a ski school chaperone, and PTA president. After the accident forced his retirement, he began devoting much of his time to the Senior Center.

He raised funds for the Center by recycling metal, getting elected Vashon's unofficial mayor, and hawking pesto salmon sandwiches at the Strawberry Festival. He served eight years on the Center Board. And he continues to organize Monday night bridge play and volunteer for Neighbor to Neighbor.

"Helping others gives you great satisfaction," George says, "and you learn a lot along the way."

George Eustice, Vashon's Santa Claus, and Mrs. Claus, his wife, Sandy.

HELP PEOPLE
Mike Quenneville

After a lifetime of helping others, Mike Quenneville found himself needing help. He uses a walker to get about and depends on his wife, Nancy, to manage his day.

"What was important to me was helping others," says Mike, a short, congenial fellow, "and now I'm being helped."

It's an unexpected role reversal for this father of five, who volunteered much of his free time to assist others. For years, he was active in Vashon Kiwanis, serving as president and leading the local program to address unmet needs of preschool children. He lobbied lawmakers in Olympia and Washington, DC, for Results, a national, grassroots anti-poverty movement. And on the island, he has long served with the St. Vincent de Paul Society, helping people in emergency situations with rent, food, and utilities.

One of eight children raised by French Canadian parents in Windsor, Ontario, Mike's first language was French. At school, he was a good athlete. He boxed (welterweight) and made the all-city high school football team as a 145-pound lineman. Following graduation, he enlisted in the Air Force, which sent him to Biloxi, Mississippi, where he learned electronics and met Freda at a USO dance. They married soon after.

Mike's Air Force training led to electronics jobs in Indiana and, in 1961, to Boeing, where he worked on airborne radar systems. He and Freda had four children, whom they raised on Seattle's Capitol Hill. Although the marriage ended, Mike later helped Freda struggle with cancer until her death.

In 1980 he married Nancy, whom he'd met in a tai chi class. They had a daughter, Renee, and moved to Vashon in part so Mike could ease his commute to Boeing. As backup driver on the Metro van, he was known for a sharp traffic eye for making the 4:30 pm ferry. He no longer drives but he still helps out by singing in the church choir and serving food at the Community Meal.

Mike Quenneville served in the US Air Force.

78

IF IT'S BROKE,
IT'S FIXABLE
Jim Dam

Jim Dam might have spent his life fixing Pontiacs in his dad's garage in Tyler, Minnesota if the school superintendent hadn't grilled him one day about college. "I was reasonably adept at car repair and it seemed satisfying at the time," Jim recalls. "But the superintendent didn't want to hear that."

So Jim, the oldest son in a family of eight, headed off to a Danish Lutheran college in Des Moines, Iowa. Two years later he transferred to South Dakota State, where he majored in physics. He had a job at Boeing in Seattle before he graduated.

Jim credits his good fortune to being born in 1936 at the height of the Depression. His graduation classes were small and job recruiters were hungry. Before he officially graduated, he was part of a Boeing test data group for the Minuteman Missile.

A soft-spoken, unflappable fellow, Jim chuckles about his 36-year career at Boeing. "I was there 26 years before I got to work on an airplane," he says. First it was the Minuteman. Then it was a fun but unprofitable Boeing project to build hydrofoils. The commercial Jetfoils found their way to Hong Kong, where they still ferry passengers to Macau. Finally Boeing assigned Jim to airplanes. His group was tasked with subjecting the 767 and its successors to all sorts of tests, including making sure a jet with two engines could fly and land with one.

"It was very enjoyable work," Jim says. It ended in 1995, when Boeing offered Jim a buyout for early retirement. He and his wife, Edna, moved to Vashon, where Jim was soon managing the bridge club and serving as secretary-treasurer of the Interfaith Coalition on Homelessness (IFCH). Through IFCH and the Lutheran Church, he helps the Island's homeless secure food, housing, and treatment services. "I hope we can make life a little better for these people," he says.

One of Jim Dam's many jobs in a long engineering career at Boeing was monitoring the instruments in a test Jetfoil boat.

INCLUDE EVERYONE
Wendy Wharton

Ever since a car-bicycle collision left her son David with a traumatic brain injury, Wendy Wharton has been on the lookout for kids on the highway. When she and David spot a helmeted kid riding a bike, they pull over their car, thank the child for wearing a helmet, and reward the youngster with one of the dollar bills they keep ready in the glove box.

A while ago, Wendy and Spider Macleod, owner of Spider's Ski & Sports, began "Lites for Tykes." Spider supplied the bright lights for mounting on bikes or arms. And Wendy handed them out to kids she found walking or pedaling on Vashon roads on dark evenings.

Preventing accidents that cause brain injuries is only part of Wendy's crusade. The other half is including people who have suffered severe brain injuries--like her son David. She encourages others to welcome and include the "differently abled" to meetings, social events, and gatherings. She and David meet monthly with a group of islanders, mostly Unitarians who have responded to their church's challenge to welcome everyone. They call themselves the Inclusion Group. They work to identify and overcome the barriers that exclude the physically and mentally disabled.

A retired registered nurse, Wendy has spent a lifetime helping the ailing and the vulnerable. Born in Fort Collins, Colorado, she grew up in Afghanistan, New Zealand, Bermuda, and elsewhere, because her father was in the US Foreign Service. She finished high school in Virginia, moved back to Colorado, married, raised four children—mostly as a single mother—and worked in hospitals in Denver and Boulder, in maternity and cancer care.

In 1995 she moved to Ojai, California, to care for her aging parents. After her mother died, she took her elderly father to Vashon so she could tend to him as well as assist her son, JB, with a new baby. Son David joined her in 2009.

Welcome and include
the differently abled.

INNOVATE
Tim Carney

Tim Carney was a fourth grader in Fontana, California, when two events thrust him into a lifelong fascination with art and science. One day a teacher brought an oversize art book to class and showed her students "The Persistence of Memory," the iconic painting by Salvador Dali. Against a barren landscape, limp clocks melt on a desk, a tree limb, and a sleeping creature. "My jaw dropped and my mind caught fire," Tim recalls. "I was so astounded that an artist could create an alternative reality."

Tim was awestruck again when he saw a fellow student fire up a homemade, 6-foot, 1.5 million volt Tesla Coil that unleashed two-foot lightening bolts. He became captivated with electricity, magnetism, metals, and applied science. In junior high, he began painting acrylics on rocks and eventually progressed to the use of holographic metallic foils that produce a dazzling luminescence. He was in love with science and art.

The oldest of four born to a millwright and a homemaker, Tim followed his father into Kaiser Steel's Fontana plant, where he worked as a crane operator pouring molten iron into open hearth furnaces. The work inspired his creativity. He built a carbon arc furnace to experiment with art materials. He filled sketchbooks with drawings of paintings he hoped to do and machines he wanted to build.

Tim married, had a daughter, and moved to Riverside, California, where it looked as if his art career was taking off. He got a commission to do a huge mural for a corporation. Art museums bought his painted rocks. He had a studio. But depression and alcohol undid him. His marriage ended and he hit rock bottom.

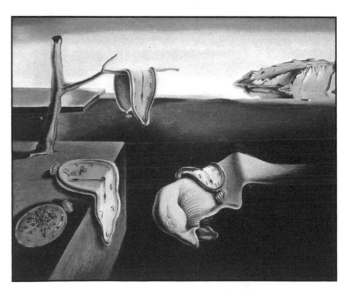

Salvador Dali's painting, "The Persistence of Memory," astounded Tim Carney.

In 2010, Tim moved to Vashon. "Drinking had made me a recluse," he says. He got active in the 12-Step Movement, detoxed, found a cabin in the woods and a community of friends. He reads copiously, still looking for methods to enhance his art. Google "Tim Carney's art portfolio" and you can see it.

IT'S YOUR LIFE
Penny Kimmel

Penny Kimmel's great-great-grandfather came to the island in 1885. Her grandfather opened a grocery in Vashon town in 1923. Her dad built the IGA store there in 1959. And her mom, now divorced, raised Penny and her three brothers and managed the store. Penny was a cashier.

An indifferent student partial to partying, Penny got a big jolt at 17. Her father, grandfather, and brother Pat died within months. Dealing with her grief, Penny retreated into meditation. "I got into the existentialism of life," she says. She was on a new journey.

You're the author of your life, and every day is a new page.

She did colleges—Highline, Tacoma, Central Washington University. In between she drove her camper to San Francisco, where she lived in a group flat next to the Panhandle, studied astrology, watched the Grateful Dead practice, and earned an FCC TV engineer license. Ultimately, she was back on Vashon, checking at mom's store, when conversations with two customers who were KIRO-TV managers led to a job at the TV station. The hours were deadly (3 pm–12 am), the macho environment toxic, and the commute exhausting. Yet Penny loved the work. She edited PSAs and ran live studio camera on news and entertainment shows, including JP Patches. She married the "audio guy," had a son, and bought her mom's house on Vashon.

The long hours and late commute didn't work with marriage or mothering. Penny quit KIRO, divorced, and found work that gave her parenting time. She drove a school bus, managed a gift shop, ran a storage facility, and videotaped weddings and dance performances. An accomplished seamstress, she did specialty work including a turquoise and pink Velcro body suit designed to keep flies off a horse's belly. The horse wore it in the Strawberry Festival parade.

Her son older, Penny returned to work in Seattle, facilitating cable TV public access shows. She helped community groups do live music, comedy, arts, and interview shows. "It was my best job," she says. But in 2010 the city slashed funding, and Penny moved to Seattle University to teach video production until retiring in 2016. "You're the author of your life," says Penny, explaining hers, "and every day is a new page."

JUBILATION
Hal Green

Hal Green notes that the Spanish word for retirement is "jubilación." Jubilation. Which is what he feels about his two decades of retirement. Why? 1) He married Molly and returned to Vashon. 2) The newlyweds rehabilitated Triplebrook, his father's historic farm where, as a boy, he lay on his back gazing up into the same night sky that had mesmerized ancient peoples. 3) He rekindled his childhood fascination with ancient civilizations by immersing himself in the astronomy of the Maya. He joined an archeological dig in Guatemala, participated in archeology conferences in the US and Europe, and wrote a chapter of the book *Archaeoastronomy and the Maya*.

Euphoria in retirement came naturally to Hal, a vigorous, passionate fellow whose life wound through several vocations and took him around the world. The older of two children adopted at birth by a timber industry executive and a homemaker, Hal grew up happily on Seattle's Capitol Hill after a three-year interlude on the Vashon farm. He graduated from Roosevelt High School and earned BS and MS degrees at Stanford and Cornell in chemical engineering. He married a fellow Stanford student he met in a ski conditioning class.

Standard Oil recruited Hal for a research engineer job in Richmond, California, but he grew frustrated with the corporate culture. He and his wife volunteered for the Peace Corps and were assigned to teach at a secondary school in a Nigerian village. No running water, intermittent power, and 200 students ready to sing, dance, and celebrate. "It was life-changing," Hal says.

With the assignment ended, he won admission to Harvard Law School. Degree in hand, he joined a small Seattle firm that championed immigration, civil rights, and labor issues. His time there (31 years) lasted longer than his marriage. Single, yet jointly responsible for four kids, he included them in peace-building travels to the USSR. At the height of the Cold War, he co-founded Ploughshares, former Peace Corps volunteers who headed a citizens' initiative that built a Peace Park in Seattle's sister city of Tashkent, Uzbekistan. The park includes 10,000 peace tiles hand-made by school children.

Today the Soviets are gone. As are the Maya kings. But the stars that illuminated their night skies continue to shine on Hal's "jubilación."

Hal Green returned to Central Asia several times in the 1980s to work on the Peace Park in Tashkent, Uzbekistan.

JUMP IN
Keith Putnam

Keith Putnam, a jovial, retired architect with a mischievous twinkle in his eye, delights in jumping into things he knows nothing about.

When the Army sent him to Korea as a second lieutenant in the Signal Corps, it needed a defense counsel for soldiers facing court martials. Keith jumped in. His best defense, he recalls, chuckling, was getting charges against a soldier for rape, theft, and assault on a military police officer reduced to "off-limits after hours." It turned out the woman was a consenting prostitute. The thieving soldier was so drunk he had passed out. And the MP, who weighed 300 pounds, had apprehended the soldier by sitting on him. Where was the crime?

The middle child of a Puget Power manager and a homemaker, Keith came to Vashon at age six, graduated from the high school, and earned a degree in architectural engineering at Washington State. "The architect," he says, approvingly, "tells the engineer what to do." He jumped into architecture bigtime. For 50 years, mostly self-employed, he designed schools, homes, and businesses, including the K2 factory and Thriftway.

Forty-three of those years were with Martha Stewart, a teacher he married within days of helping her haul wood on Shawnee Beach. They had three sons. When Martha died in 2007, Keith was adrift.

Over 60, Puget Sound area, likes sailing.

He decided he'd try to meet a woman on the Internet. He advertised for "over 60, Puget Sound area, likes sailing." The website did a poor job filtering. "I got big, buxom babes from New York City," he laughs. The next website produced a woman who met Keith, then stepped aside to call police on her cell phone. She gave the cops Keith's name, description, and license plate number and suggested they come looking for her after three hours.

A third website introduced him to Maureen Emenegger, a widow living in Vancouver. Keith drove there, met her for coffee, and they talked for seven hours. A year later, she moved into his Shawnee Beach home. "We're a very modern couple," Keith says.

KEEP ACTIVE
Carol Slaughter

On a rainy summer day a half-century ago, you might have seen Carol Slaughter in the frigid waters of Tahlequah Beach, teaching the neighborhood kids how to swim.

"I charged 25 cents a lesson," she recalls, "and their parents kept me afloat with coffee and bourbon."

Six feet tall, long-limbed and vigorous, Carol stands out. She also stands up. She stands up for seniors, the mentally ill, the infirm, and the forgotten. She especially stands up for girls. She joined Girl Scouts the day after Pearl Harbor and has been a scout ever since. She's currently assistant troop leader and cookie chief for the girls sponsored by the Senior Center.

Scouting has been a natural complement to her long career in recreation. Born in Boston and educated in convent school, she completed a PE degree at Tufts and came west to be athletic director at Annie Wright School in Tacoma. She later worked as recreation director at the Tacoma YWCA and as a recreation therapist at Western State Hospital. She has taught gymnastics, sailing, folk dancing, and numerous sports. She's rowed around Vashon three times, once in the rain with five other moms and 11 kids. She also skis, kayaks, canoes, hikes, and crochets bags made from recycled plastic.

The brightly colored bags help raise funds for Grave Concerns, a cause Carol embraced when she heard about the thousands of unnamed graves in the semi-abandoned Western State Hospital Cemetery in Steilacoom. The volunteer group replaces numbered markers with etched gravestones. "We hear from people all over the world grateful that their loved ones are identified and remembered," she says.

Carol and her husband, Al, still live on the Tahlequah beach property where she taught swimming to their two children and the neighbor kids. Although they've traveled the world (63 countries and all seven continents), Vashon is where the heart is.

Girl Scouts®

KEEP MOVING
Chaim Rosemarin

Chaim Rosemarin, who has been an actor, director, student revolutionary, social worker, kibbutznik, and editor of scholarly journals, has led a Shakespearean life. To quote the bard, "one man in his time plays many parts."

The younger of two boys born to a union organizer and a dress factory worker, Chaim grew up in West New York, New Jersey, an immigrant community on the Hudson River. As a boy, he wondered when he would "stop speaking English and start talking Yiddish like grandma." In school, he was bookish, excelling in English, history, and debate. He earned a BA at Rutgers and an MFA in theater at Wisconsin. How he loved the stage! "I played Hamlet and Hamlet won," he says. "I thought I was Laurence Olivier."

In 1966 love and revolution were in the air. Chaim and his student bride married at the campus Hillel and marched from the ceremony to a takeover of the administration building. "We spent our wedding night in the clink." Then it was back to New York, where Chaim was a social worker in the South Bronx. After arriving one day to find his client stone dead with a needle in his arm, he applied to the UW's graduate theater program. He and his wife drove west in a red Triumph.

But politics soon superseded theater. He joined Students for a Democratic Society, demonstrated at the 1968 Democratic Convention, and raged against capitalism and imperialism. And when the cause turned sour, he divorced, left the UW, and spent

Chaim Rosemarin as Scrooge in "A Christmas Carol" in 2011.

three years on an Israeli kibbutz, melding socialism and Judaism. By 1977 he was back in Seattle, cobbling together a living as an actor, director, and theater critic. On May 18, 1981, in response to a personal ad, he met Trudy, an attractive Swiss blonde, at the Red Robin for lunch. "We had a summer fling," Chaim chuckles, "and we've been flinging ever since."

He moved in with her on Vashon and married. Chaim began acting and directing with Drama Dock. His UW connections led to a new career as an associate editor of scholarly publications. Editing cosmology articles in *The Astronomical Journal* rekindled his Jewish consciousness. He joined a Torah group, studied Maimonides, and found no contradiction between science and religion. Plus, Chaim enthuses, "It's fun to be Jewish."

KEEP ON GOING
Doug Tuma

There's no straight line between Pineville, Louisiana, where Doug Tuma grew up with four brothers and a sister on 40 acres of pine woods, and Vashon, where he cleared 10 acres, planted 500 fruit trees, and designed and built a house for a wife and two kids. In between, Doug abandoned the clarinet, mastered geometry and trig, fell into landscape architecture at LSU on a buddy's word, and got commissioned out of Navy ROTC as an ensign on a mine-detecting ship during the Vietnam War.

After the Navy, Doug figured he had two choices: Go back to Pineville, where dad ran an auto body shop and mom made delectable cream puffs, or tour the world. He took the world. He drove to New York City, boarded the Queen Elizabeth II to the UK, and gallivanted around Europe for nearly a year. He fell in love with a fellow traveler. The two took a steamer to Mexico, married in Veracruz, and arrived in New Orleans with a dollar and change.

Doug found a landscape architecture job in Houston. Within a year, however, the newlyweds were on the road again. They ran out of money in Seattle, where Doug, an agreeable fellow with a ready smile, talked his way into a job with Richard Haag, the iconoclastic UW professor who turned landscape architecture on its head. Rather than tear down the rusted machinery, boilers, pipes, and catwalks of the city's abandoned Lake Union gas works, Haag said: Let's incorporate them into a park. He and Doug pitched the radical idea at numerous public meetings and finally won the job. Doug became project manager of what became Gas Works Park, one of Seattle's biggest attractions.

"It was an unusual project," says Doug, who helped develop unusual solutions like sealing the property's severely contaminated soil with wood chips from a Ballard mill and treated sewage sludge from Metro. "It was a great mix for tomatoes."

Eventually Doug opened his own landscape design business in his Vashon home. Divorced, he met and married Kathleen Merano in 1994 and had a son. The threesome embraced the farm life, growing their own food. Doug made cider, wine, and jam, most of which he gave away. "It's a good life," he says. "It keeps me going."

A landscape architect, Doug Tuma was the project manager on Seattle's iconic Gas Works Park.

LEARNING IS FOR LIFE
Lawrence Dean

Lawrence Dean, a retired physics teacher, is insatiably curious. On clear nights you might find him with a telescope at the Maury Island overlook, scanning the heavens for stars.

Lawrence grew up on a farm just north of Detroit. After earning a master's degree in biochemistry at the University of Michigan, he headed west. In the mid-'60s, Lawrence found himself teaching high school physics in California. At one point he took a break to tutor engineering students in the Philippines.

Science is developing so fast that many books are out of date by the time they're published.

Over his long career in education and science, Lawrence especially loved teaching physics to ninth graders. He introduced his 14-year-old students to telescopes he had built at home and taught many of them how to build their own. If the science got to be too dense, he would entertain a bewildered class by reading poetry or telling stories. He was forced to retire from full-time teaching in 2005 after a detached retina left him partially blind.

In 2015 Lawrence moved to Vashon to be with his daughter and son-in-law. The island enchanted him. The music. The art. The easy walk from his condo in Vashon town to virtually any place he might want to go. He found camaraderie at the Senior Center, where he lunches regularly, participates in field trips, and surfs the Internet to read scientific journals and magazines.

"It's the only way to keep up," he says. "Science is developing so fast that many books are out of date by the time they're published."

At quiet times, Lawrence writes in his journal, a life-long practice. You'll find his occasional letters in the *Beachcomber*. The tone is positive, finding joy in the new things he's learning. For example, he reports wandering into town on a rainy Halloween night to find scores of costumed parents and children trick-or-treating local merchants. "Some were so cute I had to laugh out loud," Lawrence wrote. "Even the dogs were well-dressed."

LEARNING THROUGH TECHNOLOGY
Jake Schlumpf

The light went on for Jake Schlumpf, a middle school science teacher, when a futurist told the school district's assembled educators: "If you don't learn about computers, you're nuts." The futurist, the event's keynote speaker, then promptly sat down.

The brief speech made such an impression on Jake that he left the classroom and leapt into educational technology. He wanted to know: How can teachers best use computers to teach? And how can students best use computers to learn? It was 1980, and the only computer in the school was an old Apple 3 used for scheduling classes. At Vashon's McMurray Middle School, Jake pushed the district to invest in computers and a technology curriculum. He discovered that some kids, indifferent to conventional learning, were "liberated" by computers. They came alive.

The oldest of five kids born to a door company owner and a homemaker, Jake was barely alive at birth. Two months premature, he weighed a pound and spent his first month in an oxygen tent. He grew up in a rental house in Fife, where the family ate green bean soup, went to Mass on Sunday, and worked. His first job was bunching radishes for 45 cents an hour. Smart and clever, Jake won a scholarship to Bellarmine High School in Tacoma, where he organized rock 'n' roll dances and excelled in Latin and science.

He continued studying Latin and science at the University of Washington but dropped out his junior year to go fishing in Alaska. He fell in love with Pam McMahan when the couple helped paint a friend's house on Vashon. They bought an old house in Burton and started a family (two daughters). Jake cooked nights at the Spinnaker restaurant and returned to the UW to earn a teaching certificate. After a first teaching job in Walla Walla, he was hired by McMurray.

His enthusiasm for computer learning, however, led to an educational technology job in Bremerton, followed by one in Shoreline, where he created a fiber optic highway linking the district's schools. Apple then hired him to help teachers maximize student learning through technology. Over the years, Jake worked at computer and Internet companies in Houston, Philadelphia, Seattle, and Cambridge, Massachusetts. He was a "solutions manager," bridging the gap between techies and educators so we all learn better.

Jake Schlumpf designed the first computer curriculum at McMurray Middle School.

TALK ABOUT DEATH
Carol Spangler

When Carol Spangler moved to Vashon 15 years ago, she absolutely knew what she was going to do. "I knew the next chapter of my life would be about death and dying," says Carol, a resourceful, energetic retiree on fire about a subject most folks avoid.

Back East in Maryland and Washington, DC, she'd recruited medical personnel for Appalachia, worked in maternal and child health for county and state, served as an executive director for United Way, run a consulting business on strategic planning and management, and directed development for a foundation committed to affordable housing in inner cities. She had a BS in food & nutrition from Cornell, a master's in public health from the University of North Carolina, and a master's from Johns Hopkins in organizational management and community change. But dying? And death? Not so much.

Starting fresh, however, was not new to Carol. A daughter of Polish immigrants, she grew up in a large Catholic family of aunts, uncles, grandparents, and cousins on a small farm outside Buffalo, New York. "I didn't have friends," she says. "I had family and a magical childhood."

A self-described "super-duper late bloomer," she graduated from St. Mary's High School and enrolled at Cornell, thinking she might become a nun. She phoned her mom to tell her the news and both parents abruptly showed up at her dorm and begged her to finish college first. She did. And joined the Peace Corps, which sent her to Honduras.

After that, Carol says, "I had planned to travel the world." Instead she met Bob Spangler in an elevator. They celebrate their golden jubilee this year.

Once on Vashon, Carol began training with Providence Hospice, visited a morgue and a crematorium, and sat with the dying and their families. She completed a two-year certification program at the Sacred Art of Living & Dying Center in Bend, Oregon. And then helped create "A Vashon Conversation for the Living about Dying," using film, art, and workshops to help islanders talk about death as a natural part of life. "Life has a real spiritual thread," Carol says, "that manifests itself when you're dying."

Life has a real spiritual thread that manifests itself when you're dying.

LIFE CAN TURN ON A DIME
Dave Rogers

Three years ago Dave Rogers got hit hard. His mother and father died within months of each other. Cancer claimed his girlfriend. And then, trying to stop a roof leak, he fell and landed on his back. His vertebrae and several ribs were broken. "You can be very healthy," Dave says, "and then something can happen and that's the end of it."

Dave is back on his feet again, volunteering to do what he loves: lobbying. A member of the county advisory council on aging and disability, he's frequently in Olympia, advocating for the most vulnerable. This session he's pushing for legislation that would include hearing aid coverage for folks on Medicaid.

You can be very healthy and then something can happen.

Friendly and sociable, Dave is also clever. He once persuaded a key legislator to support exempting state employees from a disclosure requirement that would have publicized their home phone numbers. He assembled a group of young women schoolteachers, trotted them into the lawmaker's office, and suggested, "How would you like Jack the Ripper to have your daughter's phone number?" The legislator got the point.

Dave is the oldest of seven born into a working-class family in West Seattle. He attended Holy Rosary School, Seattle Prep, and Seattle University, and completed a college degree at the University of Washington at age 40. He worked as a mail sorter, health inspector and air pollution control enforcer before landing a lobbying job for the state association of port districts. His business card read: "Dave, lobbyist." He had a house close to the Capitol Building in Olympia.

But he also occupies the Vashon beach cabin where he and various family members have lived for 52 years. The commute and the long hours wreaked havoc on home life, however. His first and second marriages, with six kids between them, ended in divorces. He regrets being an absent father.

Yet, there on his living room wall is a portrait of a granddaughter. She's a lobbyist. In Washington, DC.

LIVE BOLDLY
Midge Grace

Midge Grace, a feisty, straight-talking ex-Marine corporal, was an ardent feminist long before feminism became a popular cause.

"I married six times," she says, "including marrying the third husband twice." But each time, she got tired of "being demoted to a second-class citizen" and the marriage ended. Nonetheless, Midge's husbands took her all over the globe. She's lived on both coasts, in Canada (twice), and in Africa. Born the oldest of six children to a West Virginia accountant and a homemaker, she credits her wanderlust to reading her parents' complete collection of Zane Grey westerns.

"I had to marry to get out of West Virginia," Midge says. When husband No. 1 joined the U.S. Army in 1941, she joined the Marines. She was assigned to a stateside motor transport division where she drove trucks, heavy equipment, and even two tanks.

After the war and her first two marriages ended, Midge found herself with husband No. 3 (later No. 5) in Socorro, New Mexico where she eventually taught art at New Mexico Tech. She loved painting. "Landscapes, flowers, portraits, nudes, seasons—I like to paint them all."

Even so, Midge was looking for more. She deeply desired a heightened awareness of herself and her place in the universe. She and No. 3 experimented with meditation, peyote, and Eastern religion. And then one day she found it in a chance conversation with an Indian swami in the back seat of a Volkswagen bug in Albuquerque.

He told her: "Live boldly, love your spiritual self, sin spontaneously." Now 94, she took it as her personal maxim.

In 2006, Midge moved from New Mexico to Vashon to live on a five-acre farm next door to her only child, a daughter. She's easy to spot on Fridays at the Vashon Bridge Club. Except for St. Patrick's Day, she always wears purple.

Live boldly, love your spiritual self, sin spontaneously.

LIVE FULLY AND INTENTIONALLY
Beth White

You could say that Beth White enjoys a grateful satisfaction today because of three key decisions: her year at Garfield High School, a career in social work, and her acceptance of cancer.

"I feel incredibly fortunate," says Beth, a lively, optimistic retired therapist who organizes street dances in front of her Lisabeula home. "I live life very fully and very intentionally."

I feel incredibly fortunate.

The youngest of four children born to a proper Bostonian mom and a fun-loving dad who owned a lumber company, Beth grew up in a comfortable Seattle home that valued hard work, the outdoors, and tennis. She and her siblings summered on Bainbridge Island and went to elite private schools. Except for Beth, who switched to inner-city Garfield for her sophomore year.

"It was wonderful," she says, "a great big school with Blacks, Asians, Motown music in the lunchroom — I saw the world." Yet, honoring a promise to her parents, she finished high school at St. Nicholas Girls School and went to all-women's Goucher College in Baltimore. Still, what she had experienced at Garfield stuck with her. She transferred to Ohio State, where she earned bachelor's and master's degrees in social work. "I wanted to be a clinical therapist," she says.

She succeeded. For 42 years, Beth did psychotherapy. She worked with street kids in Seattle, led a drop-out prevention program on the island, and directed Vashon Youth and Family Services. After her first marriage fell apart, she traveled abroad for a year and took stock of herself. Her encounters with world religions led her to meditation and Unitarianism. Returning to Vashon, she bought a home, helped lead the Unitarian Fellowship, and set up her own counseling practice. She loved it. She found it an incredible honor to be trusted with the most intimate and vulnerable parts of people's lives. "It was heartfelt and transformative," she says.

Her life had its own transformations. She remarried, adopted a daughter, and divorced. In 2013, Beth and Rik Muroya, a trauma therapist, fell in love and moved in together. That same year, she was diagnosed with blood cancer. Effective medical treatment has kept the cancer at bay. "I'm healthy, fit, and physically active, blessed with family, friends, and community," Beth says. "Cancer has no active presence in my life."

MAKE IT BETTER
CC Stone

At age 34, CC Stone sold a struggling Lake Tahoe restaurant that she and a partner had purchased with winnings on a horse-racing bet, and moved back to Springfield, Massachusetts. She had $100 and two trash bags of belongings.

The daughter of a utility company manager and a homemaker, CC wed at 18 rather than go to Yale, but after seven years the marriage had run its course. She moved to Tahoe to ski by day and run a restaurant by night. The horse race payoff was enough "to buy a little dive bar" and learn all about marketing. For example, don't give a bar a name ("The Metropolitan Improvement Company") that sounds like a home remodeling business. Don't expect to sell drinks in a town where casinos give them away for free. And, most importantly, understand the market and make it work for you.

An animated, enthusiastic organizer, CC returned to Springfield ready to apply what she'd learned. She teamed up with a friend to expand a restaurant. That led to a job promoting a small chain of eateries. Soon she was teaching brokers at Kidder, Peabody & Co. how to craft their sales pitches. Then she was selling sports display advertising.

Will you help me sell recycled paper packing tubes?

It all came together after she met Andy Niss on her best friend's 40th birthday. They hit it off. Several months later, CC was expecting him to say, "Will you marry me?" Instead, he asked, "Will you help me sell recycled paper packing tubes?" CC said, "Yes." She quickly realized that the key to his small family business was providing service and delivery better and faster than the big boys. It worked. The business boomed.

CC and Andy married and, six years later, sold the business to a national competitor and retired. After chancing across Vashon on a ferry ride, they bought a home on the Burton Peninsula. Their other home—a frequent vacation-stay raffle item for nonprofits—is a houseboat in Amsterdam.

MAKE SOMETHING NEW
Greg Burnham

Greg Burnham doesn't call himself an artist. "I'm just a guy who makes stuff," he says of his artistic creations. "And I like to make stuff I haven't seen before." Greg's stuff includes paintings, bamboo sculptures, collages of time pieces, bowling pins, and math formula blocks as well as human figurines amidst egg shells, Cheetos, and chess pieces. (Visit gabstudios.weebly.com)

The youngest of five kids born to a homemaker mom and a retail businessman, Greg grew up in a bookish, musical, happy home in Batavia, Illinois. He started college at a conservative school in Iowa but transferred to Beloit, a free-thinking college in Wisconsin, where he majored in English composition and made abstract Super 8 films. During the "field term" he hitchhiked to San Francisco, where he taught in a free school. Back at Beloit, he fell in love with Susie Kalhorn, the soda jerk at the student union building and now his wife of 43 years.

After her 1978 graduation, the couple packed their belongings into a green Pontiac Tempest and drove west. A distant relative had offered a beach cabin in Burton. Susie found a job. Greg painted, sculpted, wrote short stories and "Eyeland," a pseudonymous column in the *Beachcomber*. In the '80s, they dwelt in various beach cabins, a chicken house, and a brick farmhouse. After the birth of their only child and construction of their own home in the woods of Maury Island, the combination of Susie's job and making stuff wasn't quite covering the bills. Greg needed paid work.

A gas station encounter put him onto a job at the Vashon Sewer District. He started by mowing the lawns, advanced to lab tech, and eventually became the primary operator of the island's wastewater treatment plant. "It was a perfect fit for me," he says. Good pay and benefits. Personal autonomy. A contribution to society. He dubbed it "The Experienced Water Project," given what the water had gone through. He was there 25 years.

In life, whether treating sewage or making art, Greg regards mistakes as "opening the way to something new." Ponder that when you see his stuff.

Greg Burnham's mixed media piece titled "Your Move."

MAMMALS FASCINATE
Ellen Kritzman

A compelling interest in animals took Ellen Kritzman on a life journey that included cataloging biology books at the Library of Congress; writing a master's thesis on two species of mice; breeding, raising, and judging pygmy goats; and serving as Curator of Mammals at the Slater Museum of Natural History in Tacoma.

She has been on wildlife trips to see pandas in China, mountain gorillas in Rwanda, lemurs in Madagascar, and polar bears at Hudson Bay. Animals have been a constant since childhood.

The younger of two girls born to urban parents who moved from New York City to a three-acre property on Long Island, Ellen remembers chickens, ducks, pigs ("very intelligent"), and a World War II "victory garden." Her lawyer father commuted to the city and she had no friends within walking distance. She found solace in reading. At 14, she went off to Miss Hall's School, an all-girls boarding academy in the Berkshires. Her Jewish parents had cut off family ties and hidden their ethnicity for fear their daughters would suffer discrimination. "It would have so enriched my life to know my heritage and my relatives," says Ellen.

An honor student, Ellen went on to Radcliffe College, where she majored in biology. She was fascinated by species evolution, biological adaptation, and vertebrate paleontology. But the lab tech jobs she did after graduation proved disappointing: injecting cancer cells into the cheek pouches of anesthetized hamsters in chemotherapy experiments and chopping off tadpole tails in regeneration studies.

Ellen Kritzman with her prize-winning buck in a National Pygmy Goat Association show.

She started grad school in zoology at UC Berkeley but finished with a master's in library science and the Library of Congress job. She later moved to Seattle for a job at the University of Washington Library. In 1973, Ellen and her partner, Jeanne, bought acreage on Vashon for "a menagerie of animals," ultimately settling on pygmy goats.

In the early '90s, Ellen saw her job eliminated and Jeanne die. She began her "volunteer phase of life." She accompanied the Backbone Campaign to the 2008 Democratic Convention. She took on leadership roles with the Vashon Pride Alliance, Land Trust, Audubon Society, Friends of Mukai, and the Alliance for Tompotika Conservation (Google it). At the library, you can find her Guide to the Mammals of Vashon Island.

MEET YOUR NEIGHBORS
Dorothy Bauer

Dorothy Bauer was newly divorced and 61 when she came back to Vashon. She first found a cabin in the woods on the Maury Island side of Quartermaster Harbor.

But she was too shy to introduce herself to the neighbors. A first neighbor knocked on the door and invited her to phone anytime. A second neighbor fixed her water pipe — several times--after she kept puncturing it with a pick. A third neighbor jump-started her car, carried in her furniture, and offered his unvarnished opinion of a visiting "man friend."

"I loved those neighbors," Dorothy wrote in volume one of *Islanders, Meet Your Neighbors*. "It is because of them that I wanted to write this book."

Now 95, Dorothy has written seven more books about islanders of various ages, beliefs, and walks of life. There's even a governor (Booth Gardner). They share a love for the island, its beauty and its culture.

Dorothy was three when her family began summering in a canvas tent on a Quartermaster beach. She fondly remembers the day she and her three older sisters rowed around the entire island in a leaky boat that required constant bailing. "We were so free," she recalls.

Dorothy graduated from the University of Washington in social work, got married, had four children, and went back to school to study landscape architecture. She had a good job with the county's shoreline-management department but she wanted to write. She took a memoir class at the UW and then a writing workshop at the Blue Heron. She was on her way. She convinced David Hinchman, owner of Vashon Print & Design, to publish a book series about her island neighbors. Volume 1 came out in 2007.

A stroke forced her to sell her Burton home and move into Vashon Community Care. But guess what? She has a whole new set of neighbors.

Dorothy Bauer displays her profile of Gov. Booth Gardner from her seven-volume book series "Meet Your Neighbors."

MENTOR OTHERS
Steve Benowitz

Steve Benowitz, who enjoyed a career at the highest levels of the federal government, didn't start out as a great boss. He was abrasive, controlling, and hot-tempered. "I was a big ass to a lot of people," he recalls.

But gradually he learned to emulate the mentoring he'd received from wise teachers in school and helpful colleagues at work. By the time he retired, Steve had received two meritorious and one distinguished senior executive service awards from three US presidents (Bill Clinton and both Bushes).

It could not have been a better fit; it encouraged diverse viewpoints.

The third of four boys born to a Jewish family in Ogden, Utah, Steve took his father's advice and got out of town after high school. A teacher steered him to Antioch College, a small, unconventional Ohio school that alternated work with study. "It could not have been a better fit," Steve says. "Unlike UT, it encouraged diverse viewpoints." And diverse experiences. He worked at a law firm in Chicago, did research for the National Park Service, stocked the gift shop on a cruise ship, and helped develop curriculum for Philadelphia public schools. After completing a BA in history, he went on to graduate studies at Case Western Reserve University in Cleveland.

Just short of a PhD, Steve took a job with the Ohio consumer protection office, only to see the office axed by the governor. The regional Federal Trade Commission hired him to investigate consumer complaints, particularly in the car industry. Steve soon led a small team focused on automobile design defects.

He loved the work, relishing the satisfaction of winning consent agreements from car companies to correct the defects and reimburse millions to customers. The team won a $100 million settlement from Ford after discovering the automaker had made a four-cylinder engine defective by removing an oil squirt hole to save $10 a car. "It was heady stuff," Steve says.

In 1978, the FTC named him its DC personnel director, where constructive interactions and mentoring were critical. He later took a similar job at the US Treasury and then served 14 years as the personnel director at the National Institutes of Health. Retiring in 2005, Steve and his wife, Tink Campbell, moved from Virginia to Vashon.

OFFER A RIDE
Jacq Skeffington

Jacq Skeffington discovered Vashon thanks to a hitchhiker he picked up in Yellowstone Park on a summer day in 1976. Jacq was a Coast Guard officer, driving his sports car to Seattle to begin duty on the icebreaker Polar Sea. As the two approached the city, the hitchhiker persuaded Jacq to take a ferry ride and deliver him to the old Portage Store. His brother ran the store, the hitchhiker said, and Jacq could camp next door.

Jacq accepted the offer and has lived on the island ever since. Bev, a post-college sweetheart, came to the island two years later and married him. The two bought a home in Dockton and began a family.

Jacq's discovery of Vashon was as unlikely as his love for the sea. The youngest of four kids raised in an Irish Catholic home in South Orange, New Jersey, Jacq was fast and agile. He won a soccer scholarship to college, but a knee injury ended his dream of playing professionally. He graduated in philosophy and was working as "a dock rat" at a Cape May marina when a yachtsman invited him to sail to Connecticut. Once out on the ocean, his miserable allergies vanished. "I took it as a sign from the Lord," Jacq says. "I wanted to spend my life on the water."

He joined the Coast Guard and eventually became a diving officer on an icebreaker. Soon he was burying underwater cable and installing listening devices on the ocean floor. Swimming in 28-degree water, he recalls, was like wriggling through jello.

After the Coast Guard, Jacq took his navigation skills to the Merchant Marine. For much of the next 35 years, he piloted oil tankers along both US coasts and through the Panama Canal. He retired in 2013 to volunteer at the Presbyterian Church, the Senior Center, and Honoring Choices Vashon.

"Through the people I've met along the road," Jacq says, "I've had a wonderful life."

Jacq Skeffington, a Coast Guardsman, peers out of a 165-pound Navy diving rig as he prepares to do an underwater ship salvage.

OVERPERFORM
Neil Jungemann

Neil Jungemann, who broke horses as a kid and engineered radar systems as an adult, is a guy who overperforms. He arrives early to work, stays late to finish, and solves far more problems than he creates. As a result, he says, "I've never had to look for work."

He's not smug about it. Bright, positive, and good-humored, Neil attributes his good fortune to an upbringing in rural South Dakota centered on home, church, and family. His dad, a mechanic with an eighth-grade education, could diagnose engines by listening to the motor. His mom taught elementary school. Both valued education, sending all four of their children to boarding school for their junior and senior years at Bethany Lutheran High School & College in Mankato, Minnesota. As a result, Neil's high school classmates decreased in number from 4,000 in Sioux Falls to 80 at Bethany.

Although he loved physics and math (the Fibonacci numbers captivated him), Neil drifted at Bethany College. He quit for a four-year hitch in the Air Force, which trained him as an "airborne communications navigation repairman" and sent him to bases all over North America. With the service behind him, he earned a BS in electrical engineering at South Dakota State. Boeing recruited him immediately and sent him to Seattle, where he met and married Gay in 1967.

Hughes Aircraft soon lured him to engineer fighter jet radar, first at its plant in Los Angeles and later at Air Force bases worldwide. Over the next 12 years, Neil, Gay and their son, Owen, lived in three states, Canada, and Iran. Just before the fall of the shah, Neil was liaising with the Iranian military. Ultimately, Hughes asked him back to LA to reverse-engineer Soviet technology. The secretive program was conducted under close surveillance in a no-daylight vault. "Gay had no idea," Neil says.

In 1979 the family returned to Seattle and Neil to Boeing. Author Betty McDonald's Vashon adventures induced them to move to the island. Neil retired from Boeing in 1999, bringing his overperforming skills to the Rotary, the Food Bank, the community council, the bridge game, and the golf course. He'll be there before tee time.

I've never had to look for work.

PAY ATTENTION
Kate Smith

Kate Smith was a small-town teenager when she fell in love with a poet and folk artist 11 years her senior and fled Illinois forever. She'd never been on a plane, never been beyond the Mississippi, yet she'd saved $125 and California beckoned.

It was nearly the Summer of Love, and Kate and Bill Sandiford, the poet, and their musician friends were going west. They started in Los Angeles, where they worked in folk and music clubs, but their "tribe" soon migrated to San Francisco. Kate and Bill got married there and had a baby boy. The tribe moved on, first to Kansas City, where Kate and Bill lived communally in a banker's mansion, then back to LA, where the marriage fell apart.

Kate was introduced to John Smith, a hippie living in the California desert. In 1971 the two of them packed up a truck with her son, his two daughters, and their belongings—including the geese and peacocks—and drove to Vashon, where John's great-grandparents had left them a tumbledown house in Ellisport. Eventually they bought a Dockton farmhouse, where Kate gave birth to their daughter. So with their four kids, she and John staged "a big counterculture wedding." But the celebration didn't last. In 1980 John returned to California.

I stayed on Vashon because I had a community here.

"It was a very traumatic time," recalls Kate. "But I stayed on Vashon because I had a community here."

Kate waitressed on the island. But at age 40, she realized "it's a sad life to be an old waitress." She completed a BA at Evergreen State College and became a legal advocate for domestic violence (DV) victims and later a county probation officer supervising DV offenders.

Now retired, Kate calls her chaotic married life an asset because it gave her first-hand insight into both the victim and the offender. "I made my life my livelihood," she says. "Pay attention and life will point you in the right direction."

PERSEVERE
Lornie Walker

Lornie Walker, wife, mother, teacher, and writer, has had a life of perseverance. The most recent was overcoming cancer: uterine at age 53 and breast at 62. She credits her health and vigor to a "positive attitude." "I did not let cancer get me down," she says.

Earlier she persevered mightily to become a teacher. Growing up the youngest of three children in an affluent neighborhood of Buffalo, New York, Lornie struggled with an undiagnosed learning disability. Her private school put her in a reading group called "The Turtles." Comparing herself to her bright, gorgeous, and talented adopted sister, who was a mere year older, Lornie developed a "disastrous self-image." She finished high school and went to an all-girls junior college in Washington, DC, where she was told teaching was beyond her. She majored in "executive secretarial" and became an office assistant.

A decade later, she was working as a classroom aide in Stanwood when her colleagues convinced her she could teach. She completed a degree in special ed, graduating magna cum laude, and was on her way. "I found myself," Lornie says. "Kids brought out a joy in me I'd never experienced before."

A third perseverance was the most difficult. Lornie had to reconcile with her family of origin: a loving but controlling mom, a distant and depressed dad, an adopted brother who drifted off to San Francisco, and, most importantly, Mary, the debutante older sister so dazzlingly beautiful that she was photographed in Town & Country. Yet, after marriage and a child, Mary had slipped into manic depression. Lornie, living in Seattle, invited her to come west and live with her. It didn't work out. In 1975 Mary lit herself on fire and jumped off the Roanoke Street Bridge. She survived but two years later jumped off the higher 12th Avenue S. bridge. It was fatal.

"I felt guilty for not saving her," Lornie says. "And for years I struggled to let it go." Eventually, through the process of writing a book, *Argyle Park: A Memoir of My Sister's Suicide*, she did let it go. She forgave her sister— and herself.

Lornie Walker, a cancer survivor, hikes in the Olympic National Forest.

PERSIST
David Cole

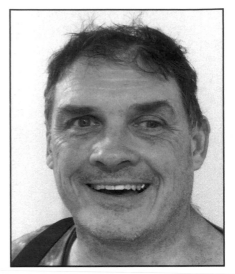

David Cole "woke up" one day from a six-month coma and discovered that Ronald Reagan was president, John Lennon had been assassinated, and he had no idea what year it was. An 18-year-old freshman at the University of Colorado, he had suffered a traumatic brain injury when a car smashed into him as he cycled near campus.

His face immobile and impassive, he had no initial recognition of family members. He had to be taught how to eat. He could not speak. Yet, inexplicably, he could write and began communicating by scribbling notes. Gradually, he recovered his speech. But other things eluded him. He needed reminders to do simple tasks like brushing his teeth.

Years of therapy ensued but David persisted. He managed to earn a degree in therapeutic recreation. He married a woman who had also suffered a severe brain injury. They had three children. It was challenging as the kids realized they had to depend on each other to help parents whose brains did not work like their own. After 14 years, the marriage fell apart.

David Cole published a book about his traumatic brain injury.

Eventually, David's brother, JB, encouraged him and their mother to come to Vashon. Their mom, Wendy Wharton, came first, and when David arrived in 2009, he moved in with her. "Mom is my roommate," David says. The two of them go weekly to therapy sessions at Vashon Youth and Family Services, where they untangle the intricacies of brain injury.

Five years ago, Wendy got Toby, a Goldendoodle, who is now David's service dog and companion. "Toby helps David socialize," Wendy says, noting that the dog encourages folks to initiate conversations with David. With Toby quietly seated at his side, he is a warmly welcomed regular at the Senior Center. And he's more comfortable venturing out, having breakfast at Sporty's, helping neighbors clear blackberries, and riding the bus to Seattle to meet with a support group of others who have suffered severe brain injuries.

PROTECT THE EARTH
Susie Kalhorn

Susie Kalhorn grew up on six acres in rural Sugar Creek, Missouri, where she developed a passion for the outdoors. Her love of nature took her on a career journey she could not have imagined as a child picking grasshoppers from her socks and carrying opossums and ringneck snakes on her bike.

The youngest of four children born to a school teacher and a Hallmark Cards executive, Susie played both basketball and the violin and was an exchange student in Germany. Still, she felt trapped by the expectations of her small home town. For college, she chose Beloit because the admission form had asked: Tell us about yourself. She did. She majored in chemistry and philosophy and did a field term at the Argonne National Laboratory, where she studied water quality in Lake Michigan.

A year later, she and her college sweetheart, Greg Burnham, were living in a Vashon beach cabin. She was bottling apple juice at the Wax Orchards farm when she landed a job as a lab tech at the UW Oceanography Dept. Soon she was on scientific expeditions studying oxygen-deprived zones at the ocean floor. The expeditions took her to reefs in Tahiti, fjords in Norway, and hydrothermal vents near the equator. On one cruise, the crew outran a hurricane. After four years of exhausting hours at sea, Susie came home to Vashon for good. She worked at Minglement while taking environmental courses at Evergreen State College.

By contacting key players, she talked herself into several government projects. She did risk assessment research on the storage of nuclear waste at Hanford. She examined habitat loss as a result of oil spills in Puget Sound. With the King County development department, she brought rural property owners together with urban environmentalists in hopes of achieving some shared goals. She might start a discussion with: "What should we do for fish?" As a consultant, Susie wrote an environmental curriculum for Vashon schools and pioneered the "Sludge Fest," a hands-on workshop about septic systems.

"Opportunities arise," says Susie, a founding member of the Land Trust, a past president of the Senior Center, and a former board member of local nonprofits. "Take them."

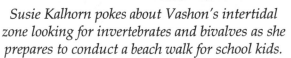
Susie Kalhorn pokes about Vashon's intertidal zone looking for invertebrates and bivalves as she prepares to conduct a beach walk for school kids.

PROVE YOUR WORTH
Mary Pekarek

In the days when folks didn't talk about sexual harassment, Mary Pekarek was in the thick of it. She was a woman Teamster driving trucks in an industry dominated by macho men who had little use for women. One supervisor demanded she arm-wrestle him for a job. Some drivers refused to talk to her. Others gave her bum information. On the job training, she laughs, "I backed up like a snake." And then there were the creeps who grabbed and groped despite her extra layers of clothes.

"One guy thought my crotch was his," recalls Mary, relishing the memory of how she got back by goosing him royally from behind. "He didn't speak to me for a year."

The second of four children born to a master mechanic and a homemaker, Mary grew up in Edina, Minnesota, attended the University of Minnesota, then quit to marry an aeronautical engineer. His job took them west to Boeing, where they raised three kids in Kent. When the marriage ended, Mary needed a good-paying job. She found it at Glacier Sand and Gravel.

A perpetually positive person incapable of holding a grudge, Mary survived the harassment and proved her worth. She was soon driving trucks to construction sites all around Puget Sound. At each site, she studied how foundations were poured, buildings framed, and plumbing and electricity installed. In 1986 she bought five acres near Burton and started building her own house. A second husband helped for a while, but the design, the framing, the sheet rocking, the whole shebang, was hers. "The building inspector couldn't believe it," she says proudly, "but I read the code books."

Mary Pekarek, a 30-year Teamster, prepares to unload a cement truck she drove for Glacier Sand and Gravel.

Today, the house, surrounded by gardens, a greenhouse, an art studio, and ongoing projects, is the center of Mary's retired life. Her son, David, and his wife, Oxana, live downstairs, and her grandson, Zhora, upstairs. "I enjoy this house being filled with people," she says, gratefully. "I love my life."

PURSUE STILLNESS
Scott Gaul

At age 19, Scott Gaul was so severely injured from crashing his hang glider that he was in a coma for four weeks. As he regained consciousness from this near-death experience, he came to the realization that a world exists beyond the physical world. He began to study meditation, went to India to study under a spiritual teacher, and learned a meditation practice that he has pursued ever since.

Daily meditation, he says, has given him "peace of mind." Today he teaches others how to use meditation to create a state of relaxation in which anxiety and stress fade away. His students include those who come to his Guided Meditation Class on Friday mornings at the Senior Center and thousands of others who watch his meditation videos online at scottgaul.com.

You have to plod along, developing the skill of working with your inner landscape.

"Meditation is a skill," Scott says. "You have to plod along, developing the skill of working with your inner landscape." His students sit in a comfortable position, close their eyes, become aware of their body sensations, concentrate on their breathing, and watch their thoughts pass by without becoming attached to them. Letting thoughts go is one of the important skills of meditation. The result—ideally—is a mind at peace.

An attentive, quiet fellow who often wears a gray tunic, Scott grew up in Bellevue after his parents moved the family from "the shadow of Disneyland." He no sooner graduated from Bellevue High School than he had a career in computer graphics. More than 20 years later he went back to school at Antioch University, where he earned a degree in spiritual studies.

"I've pursued two paths in life," he says, "technology and meditation." Along the way he's been a videographer, a hospital chaplain, an artist, a massage therapist, a computer trainer, and a volunteer firefighter. Scott, his former wife, and their son moved to Vashon two decades ago to escape the congestion on the Eastside and, well, find peace of mind.

PURSUE YOUR CALLING
Charlotte Masi

Charlotte Masi has been single-minded about life. Early on, she knew she was going to leave home, go to college, and pursue a career in commercial art and industrial design.

She attributes this determination to hardworking parents, who sold and managed self-serve laundries in the Dallas area, and maternal grandparents, who trusted, understood, and encouraged her. Her grandparents, cattle ranchers, put her on a horse shortly after she learned to walk.

Charlotte took a drafting course in middle school and another in her 4,000-student public high school. She excelled. Teachers urged her to pursue art and design in college. She did, whizzing through East Texas State University with a double major. Later, at another teacher's recommendation, she worked on a master's degree in ceramics and welded metal sculpture at Texas Women's University.

While managing a contract furniture showroom in Dallas, she seized an opportunity to design a signage system for office buildings in Saudi Arabia, which resulted in her being recruited by Architectural Signage, Inc in Los Angeles. When she drove across the California border, she knew she wouldn't be looking back. Living in Laguna Beach and working for ASI "was one of the best times of my life," says Charlotte.

Yet seven years later, suffering from a broken heart, Charlotte accepted an invitation to move to Seattle to stay with friends while she got going again. She soon landed a consulting job in Singapore doing signage for Raffles City, a huge hotel, office, and shopping complex designed by I.M. Pei. Over 10,000 signs! When the project ended, she and a fellow designer married and started their own design firm in Seattle. "Professionally, we were great together," she says, but after moving to Vashon and a foray into breeding llamas, the marriage ended.

Charlotte Masi's design consulting work for Raffles City, Singapore, produced 10,000 signs.

Charlotte then spent two years in Bellingham as an advertising art director for Haggen Food & Pharmacy, but had to leave to care for her aging parents in Dallas. Eventually, she returned to Vashon, where she resumed design work (she did The Whole Vashon Catalog) and took up gourd art and watercolor painting. It's all about art and design.

PURSUE YOUR PASSION
Alice Bloch

Alice Bloch, a retired technical writer who directs Vashon's Meals on Wheels program, has always pursued her passion. Sometimes it came with the job, but more often than not it was because she found something fascinating. Like creative writing.

Sincere and soft-spoken, Alice has had many passions in life. Her first one was foreshadowed by a dream she had as a three-year-old in her hometown of Youngstown, Ohio. The oldest of five children, she dreamt that she was pushing her baby brother in a stroller along a sidewalk. She got to a cross street, looked both ways for traffic (Alice is a cautious person), and then proceeded into the street. All of a sudden, a speeding car appeared out of nowhere, headed straight for them. Alice calmly leaned over and whispered in her brother's ear, "Don't worry. This is just a dream."

She later concluded that her ability to take herself outside her own dream suggested she had a very rational and creative mind. After university studies at Michigan, Cornell, and Hebrew University in Jerusalem, she became a writer. Her word skills took her to Los Angeles and, in 1990, to Seattle, where she retired from IBM.

Writing based on her own life fueled her passion. She published a 1981 memoir about a sister who died at 20 of leukemia. She later wrote *Mother-Daughter Banquet* about her role as a surrogate mother to her four younger siblings after their mother's untimely death at 33. And, in fiction and essays, she dealt with her experience of growing up Jewish and lesbian in the 1960s. She almost married a gay man, then thought better of it. Instead, the two founded Liberation House, a gay and lesbian drop-in center in Manhattan.

Fifteen years ago, Alice and Sharon, her spouse, moved to Vashon, where Alice developed a passion for writing about the arts. She has reviewed theater, opera, and classical music events for the *Seattle Gay News*. She and Sharon are also passionate about birds, traveling to birding areas nationally and abroad.

Alice Bloch, at 5, with brother Eddie, 2, on the beach in Atlantic City. She saved him in a dream.

As director of the island's Meals on Wheels program, Alice coordinates the delivery of prepared meals to housebound seniors. She especially enjoys visiting with ailing or disabled seniors who rarely go out. "It's extremely gratifying," she says.

PUT FAMILY FIRST
June Langland

Optimistic and positive, June Langland gives all the credit for 90 years of contentment to her family: loving parents and grandparents, an exceptional husband ("one of the best persons God ever put on earth"), her two daughters and two sons, 10 grandchildren, and 13 great-grandchildren. "If I didn't have family," she says, "I don't know what I'd do."

She was 12 when her father, a manager for Shell Oil, dropped dead of a heart attack in their Montana home. Her distraught mother packed up her and her brother and moved to their grandparents' chicken farm on Vashon. Mom started a floral business, remarried, and had a daughter as June was completing Vashon High School. Eight days after June graduated, she married Dewey Langland, a University of Washington engineering grad whom she had met at a New Year's Eve dance in Burton.

Marrying at 18 and pregnant at 19, June says, "was the best thing that ever happened to me." Why? "Because I've been able to watch kids grow up."

Yet it's been tough at times. Her oldest child required hip reconstruction at three and had polio and epilepsy. June, employed as a shipping clerk, and Dewey, with the US Corps of Engineers, worked long hours, relying on relatives to babysit, while they struggled to pay medical bills. Their daughter's health improved, and in the 1970s Dewey's job took the family to Germany and later to Saudi Arabia.

June loved both assignments. From Frankfurt, she drove sightseeing relatives around Europe. In Riyadh, confined to an American compound with armed guards at the gate, she put on a long cotton dress, headscarf, and veil, and had her Somali driver escort her to an office job forbidden to women. By computer and fax, June dealt with male secretaries to help hire US professors to teach in Saudi Arabia.

After a second stint in Frankfurt, June and Dewey returned to Vashon and plunged into retirement. Dewey bought a boat and joined the yacht club. June, a singer and pianist, served on the boards of the Lutheran Church and the Vashon Island Chorale. But mostly, it was all about family — birthdays, weddings, and celebrations. "Family," June says of herself and her late husband, "came first."

Dewey and June Langland, seated center, gather with the greater Langland family to celebrate their 65th wedding anniversary in August 2014.

READ AND LEARN
Mary Anne Nagler

Perhaps Mary Anne Nagler's passionate love of reading began with the Madeline series about Catholic girls in a Paris boarding school or maybe with the children's novel The Witch of Blackbird Pond. But by the time she graduated 15th in a senior of class of 750 at her inner-city Detroit high school, she was determined to go to library school.

It wasn't easy. Her father, a boiler operator, had died when she was nine. Her mother took a clerical job and they scraped by. Mary Anne commuted from home to attend Wayne State while working 30 hours a week as a drug store clerk. It was rough. She was held up at gunpoint, then lost the job when the store was firebombed.

After a summer learning French at the Sorbonne, she returned to Wayne State and got a job shelving books at the Detroit Library. She completed a BA in English, continued to work at the library, and met another librarian, who began a long and cautious courtship. Mary Anne, an enthusiastic go-getter, concluded that the noncommittal Richard was "not good husband material" and took a library job in Arizona.

Richard was not dissuaded. He sent her chocolates. He set up rendezvous in San Francisco, New York, and elsewhere. He took a voluntary six-month layoff to be with her in Arizona. Finally, after four years, they reunited in Detroit. A priest and a rabbi officiated at their 1985 wedding alongside a witch, an old girlfriend of Richard's.

The couple soon had two daughters, and Mary Anne was balancing the library with motherhood. In her mid-40s, she decided to quit the library and become a college instructor. She completed an MA in English and got a full-time position at a community college. She taught remedial English, essay writing, and women's literature.

When she and Richard retired in 2010, they wanted to live in the Pacific Northwest. And after a weekend stay at the farm of Betty MacDonald, whose books Mary Anne had read, they decided on Vashon.

Mary Anne Nagler studied at the Sorbonne in Paris.

READ FOR HAPPINESS
Lorna Estes

Early on, Lorna Estes discovered that with a good book she is perfectly content to stay home and read. In childhood, Nancy Drew mysteries took her to moonstone castles, moss-covered mansions, and phantoms on piney hills. Later, Joseph Conrad transported her up the Congo River into the Heart of Darkness while T.E. Lawrence — the Lawrence of Arabia — plunged her into World War I and into the deceit and folly of colonialism in the Middle East. Oh, there are so many fabulous books!

Nowadays macular degeneration has dimmed Lorna's eyesight, but with a backlit iPad she reads electronic versions of newspapers, magazines, and books. She figures she spends half her waking hours reading. "As an introvert," Lorna says, "I don't go out searching for something. I get my adventure from what I read at home each day."

The second of four children born to a Civil Service employee and a homemaker, Lorna grew up in Burton, playing in the woods, roaming the beach, and reading. At Vashon High School, she hung out in the library, learned French (which she still reads and speaks), and fell in love with Bob Estes, a football star, whom she married at 19, two years after graduation. The couple bought a home in Ellisport and had two daughters, who also became devoted readers. "The only noise in our house," Lorna jokes, "was pages turning."

To support a family, Lorna earned a cosmetology license at Bates Technical School in Tacoma, then styled hair on Vashon for nearly five decades, mostly at James' Hair

Design. She loved the "peaches and cream" smell of the beauty shop and the artistry and intimacy of touching, cutting, brushing, coloring, and styling hair. "I met wonderful people I would never have met otherwise," she says. "In fact, I'd still be cutting hair today if I could see well enough."

A regular at the Senior Center Book Club, Lorna savors stories with richly drawn characters, humorous predicaments, and adventurous plots that demand reading to the very end.

Lorna Estes and her daughter, Page, 6, read to each other in the family home in Ellisport.

RECOGNIZE OPPORTUNITY
Tom Dinsmore

Tom Dinsmore was never much interested in school, especially after discovering cars and girls. His learning came from outside the classroom. He was three weeks old when his mother died and his maternal grandparents took over. They adopted Tom, raising him on a farm near Everett and later in a North Seattle home. Grandma and grandpa were from Maine, Downeasters who retained their accents, traditional values, and hard work habits. Grandpa, a machinist for the Great Northern Railroad, taught Tom to cut cord wood, ride a horse, milk a cow, dynamite stumps, and take apart an engine.

"I was taught how to work, not to play," says Tom, a likable fellow who makes friends easily. Fortunately, he had a natural inclination for understanding how things worked.

Fresh out of Seattle's Lincoln High School, he was employed at an auto shop in Ballard when the Army drafted him and shipped him to Korea as a mechanic. Called home for his grandpa's death, Tom finished his service in the Army Reserve and married. Twenty years later, he says, "I woke up and discovered I was a bachelor with four boys; the youngest was 11." His wife had walked out.

In 1964 Tom was working at a Seattle auto shop when he got an offer to deliver propane on Vashon. He soon realized he had a chance to run the company, which was in deep debt. Nonetheless, he seized the opportunity, running the business so well he was eventually able to buy it. He loved being boss, liked his customers, and enjoyed making deliveries, setting up tanks, and repairing appliances and furnaces.

Tom Dinsmore went from delivery man to owner of Vashon Propane.

In 1989 he sold the company, settling into a comfortable retirement of boat repair, sailing, and traveling with June Polzin, his second wife.

Tom didn't learn sailing from his grandpa. But early on he became captivated with boating. He and two other guys bought an 18-foot sailboat to cruise on Lake Union. He helped found the Shilshole Bay Yacht Club, ran a sailing school that specialized in teaching women, and built the 32-foot trimaran on which he met June. "Life's been good to me," Tom says.

RECOGNIZE OTHERS
Bob Hallowell

Bob Hallowell, a retired Seattle Times executive, likes to say there are three ways to reward volunteers: recognition, recognition, and recognition.

An unassuming fellow with a warm smile and a gentle manner, Bob doesn't appear to desire any recognition at all. Yet since retiring in 1988, he has thrown himself full-time into Vashon volunteerism. He has helped people prepare their taxes, driven folks to off-island medical appointments, explained smart phones to the baffled, and, with his wife Claire, co-led a support group for caregivers. He became a master gardener and taught gardening. He joined the Senior Center Board and served as president. Nowadays he and Claire lunch regularly at the Center, where he leads the Current Events discussion.

The two of them endow a scholarship to Washington State for Vashon students. Why WSU, where as a sorority "house boy" he once led a successful strike for better pay? "Why," he says, "because WSU was a marvelous experience."

Nonetheless, Bob earned his business degree at the University of Washington and was working as a CPA at Price Waterhouse when the Times recruited him. He was instrumental in developing the Seattle Times Fund for the Needy, which raised millions of dollars for the less fortunate. He retired as vice president of finance in 1988.

Bob grew up in Seattle, where he had three paper routes, graduated from Roosevelt High School, and, for a time, managed a restaurant on Bothell Way. Between WSU and the UW, he served two years with the US Army Counter Intelligence Corps in Japan. As a tech specialist, he transmitted intercepted Soviet code to Washington, DC.

In retiring to Vashon, Bob has gone full circle. His parents purchased a cabin at Corbin Beach in 1941. For 23 years, he and Claire and their two daughters enjoyed a summer home in Tahlequah. And now they live year-round on the Corbin Beach property he remembers so fondly from childhood.

Bob Hallowell, standing far right, with his Seattle Times executive team at the Space Needle in 1970.

REINVENT YOURSELF
Bill Swartz

By his calculation, Bill Swartz has had 23 paying jobs in his lifetime. Among them: summer camp counselor in Michigan, geology curator at the Field Museum in Chicago, USGS water quality technician on the Nevada nuclear test site, US Army medical corpsman in Korea, and auto mechanic at a British car dealership in Seattle.

During the 47 years that he, his wife, Linda, and their two daughters had a 140-acre ranch in northeastern Washington, Bill grew hay and raised and sold livestock. He also toiled as a miner, a logger, a metal worker, and a master mechanic for a sawmill. In the summer, he did water and weather tests for the Forest Service. "I've reinvented myself multiple times," says Bill, a tall, rangy fellow who prizes self-sufficiency and independence.

His dad was a Presbyterian minister who became a real estate broker, and his mom, a Navy nurse who became the night supervisor at an Air Force hospital. Bill was the older of two boys. He was six when the family moved from Dayton, Ohio to a small farm nearby. Despite their modest means, Bill was sent to Cranbrook School, a coat-and-tie boys boarding academy in Bloomfield Hills, Michigan. "I had a demanding, classical education alongside the sons of Detroit's captains of industry," he says.

He discovered drawing, painting, and sculpture and decided to continue studying art at Antioch College. But once there, a course in historical geology ("the long span

Bill Swartz, working for the Forest Service, teaches seasonal staff how to use a water temperature data recorder.

of deep time") took Bill in a whole new direction. He graduated, married Linda, his college sweetheart, and registered for the draft as a conscientious objector. The Army trained him as a non-combatant corpsman.

Once free of the service, Bill and Linda began looking "for a ranch in a little valley all by itself." They found it in remote Onion Creek in Stevens County, where their daughters rode ponies to a one-room, one-teacher school. Bill had enough paid jobs "to keep me going" and plenty to do. He served on boards for schools, libraries, water conservancy, children, and the elderly while Linda worked for the Forest Service. Half a century went by. In 2015 they sold the ranch and moved to Vashon to reinvent themselves again.

RESPECT OTHERS
John Dunn

John Dunn wears a safety pin above his breast pocket. He wears it as a show of solidarity with those who have been discriminated against because of their race, ethnicity, sex, politics, disability, or religion. The safety pin says: I'm a safe person and you're in a safe place.

John's safe place is the Vashon Senior Center, where he plays bridge and mahjong, participates in the book group, avails himself of the free coffee, and enjoys the mid-day meal with the regular lunch crowd. He's so familiar with the day-to-day operations of the place that someone got the bright idea to recruit him for the Center's Board. He graciously accepted.

I enjoy life and I want others to enjoy it as well.

Born in Virginia, John was blessed with a beautiful singing voice. At 12, he sang a soprano solo at a national musical event at Constitution Hall in Washington, DC. He still sings today in the Burton Community Church Choir.

As a young man, he studied at Virginia Tech until the Army drafted him and sent him to Vietnam, where he shelled the enemy with long-range howitzers. He describes the experience as "homicide from afar." It made him an anti-war activist.

In the late '70s, an Army buddy introduced him to a Vashon woman with whom he settled down. They married, had four children—her two and boy-girl twins of their own. The marriage foundered but the twins flourished. "Neither offspring has caused a fraction of the problems their dad has," he proudly says.

John worked at K2, the ski manufacturer that was once the island's biggest employer. With retirement, he found a second home at the Senior Center, where he is quick to help make coffee, clean up after lunch, or help a novice bridge player understand the game.

"I enjoy life," he says, summing up his 70 years, "and I want others to enjoy it as well."

RIDE HORSES
Carrie Sikorski

Very early in life, Carrie Sikorski discovered that riding horses gave her a deep sense of fulfillment. "I enjoy the nonverbal connection with horses," she says, "guiding them with my body." An energetic, athletic retiree, she could race a horse around barrels or weave it through poles or get it to go where it had no interest in going.

The older child and only daughter of a Boeing labor negotiator and a homemaker, Carrie grew up on Mercer Island when it was still rural. She played tennis, participated in Young Life, mastered piano well enough to compete in state competitions, and, at age 10, owned her first horse, Shawna. She rode the aging quarter horse bareback on the island's forested trails.

Carrie pledged a UW sorority after high school. It was a poor fit. But a four-month backpacking trip through Europe became a life-changer. She visited L'Abri, a Christian retreat in Switzerland, roomed with a Gambian woman who invited her to the embassy ball, and stayed at a 75-cent orchard shack in Crete. When she returned to the UW, she was on a new path. She graduated with a BA in environmental geography.

An internship with the EPA office in Seattle led to a series of jobs at the federal agency. She worked on noise pollution, hazardous waste, and legislative relations. She loved the EPA's smart, mission-driven staff. Among them was Jamie, a water specialist, with whom she moved to Monroe so both could board horses nearby. Carrie competed in the Western Games at the Evergreen Fairgrounds and rode back country with the Trail Dusters. She and Jamie married and, in 1987, bought acreage on Vashon large enough for them, their horses, and two daughters on the way.

Carrie left the EPA to raise the two girls, teaching them and their friends the joy of riding in nearby Island Center Forest. She finished her work career helping people with disabilities succeed in business. Two years after Jamie's 2014 death, she met and fell in love with Michael O'Donnell, Vashon's computer whiz. They've made room for grandkids, dogs, and, soon, horses.

I enjoy the nonverbal connection with horses, guiding them with my body.

SAY 'YES'
Ann Irish

Ann Irish said "yes" to just about everything that came her way. She said yes to a job at 15 after her father died and her mother moved her and her two sisters to the upper floor of a house in Lakewood, Ohio. She said yes to Les Irish, a Mossyrock, Washington farm boy at MIT, when he proposed marriage during her sophomore year at Radcliffe and took her west. She managed to earn a BA and a teaching certificate by convincing the UW to say yes to correspondence courses. Years later, she was on campus to complete a PhD in history.

"If a challenge comes along," Ann says, "I try to meet it."

The eldest child of a chemical engineer and a librarian, Ann grew up in a home that loved reading and libraries. She won a scholarship to Radcliffe, where she was amazed by rich girls who didn't clean up after themselves. She met her future husband at a party after a hiking club song fest. Both were smitten, and the marriage lasted until his death in 2021.

The couple was equally enamored of Vashon, moving to the island in 1955 and soon buying a 1922 farm house on the west side. Les commuted to Boeing, and together they raised four kids. For 26 years, Ann taught at Vashon High School, mostly government, where current events made the curriculum come alive. One day she said yes to a mailbox invitation to apply to be an exchange teacher at public high schools in Japan. Her selection led to a Japanese language class at the high school and an annual exchange trip for Vashon or Minami Himeji High School students.

More invitations came. Ann said yes to a Fulbright fellowship to Indonesia and to how-to-teach-English seminars in Vietnam, Bangladesh, and Laos (four times). After retiring from teaching in 1994, she devoted herself to writing history. She wrote a biography of Joseph W. Byrns, a distant relative and Tennessee congressman who was Speaker of the House under FDR. She wrote a history of Hokkaido, Japan's northern island. And she awaits publication of her history of the islands of Puget Sound. All because she said "yes."

An exuberant student celebrates with the English class taught by Ann Irish, center, at the Lao-American College in Vientiane, Laos in 2012.

SEE THE POTENTIAL IN OTHERS
Nancy Vanderpool

Shortly after Nancy Vanderpool and her husband, Dick, retired to Vashon two decades ago, Nancy gave a Sunday sermon at the Methodist Church. She talked about beginning a new life in a new place and not knowing what would come. Yet, she said, she was confident something would. Soon after, a homeless man arrived at the church door and no one was quite sure what to do.

So, Nancy and a couple of others invited faith-based groups to work together to address homelessness on the island, and the Interfaith Council on Homelessness (IFCH) was born. Today Nancy is Vashon's best-known unpaid social worker. She helps people going through hard times find housing or keep their housing by providing funding for rent, utilities, and other bills.

I try to see the potential in people, and I build on that.

"I try to see the potential in people," says Nancy, a thoughtful woman with a wry sense of humor, "and I build on that." Sometimes it works. Some take the next step and pull their lives together. Others remain trapped in destructive behavior.

The older sister born to a home builder and a homemaker, Nancy grew up in the tiny Eastern Oregon town of Arlington. As co-valedictorian in a senior class of 12, she was soon off to the University of Oregon, where she graduated in English literature. She realized she liked college and she liked people. She won a fellowship to Syracuse University that prepared her to be a dean of women. It was a hands-on education. Nancy shared a residence cottage with a dozen freshman girls and mentored them.

In graduate school, she married Dick, with whom she'd fallen in love on a train ride to a national student assembly. They found academic jobs together at a small college in Havre, Montana, and started a family, a boy and a girl. They later moved to Corvallis, Oregon, where Nancy was assistant dean of students at Oregon State and Dick taught history in a community college. When retirement time came, they discovered Vashon.

SEE WITH NEW EYES
Wade Yip

After moving to Vashon from New York City, where he had a long career as a graphic designer and photographer, Wade Yip started a photo group at the Senior Center. It wasn't a typical class with a text, curriculum, and assignments. In fact, it's a club. Wade, a gentle, soft-spoken fellow who mirrors the mindfulness meditation he practices, says club members learn from each other and known photographers.

Aside from sharing their work, the club's activities include field trips, talks, and exhibits. Subjects range from landscape, nature, and portraits to experimental treatment of light, color, and pattern. Cameras vary from bulky digital models to sleek cell phones. The club focuses on seeing the world with fresh eyes rather than emphasizing techniques, Wade explains. (See photoclubvsc. blogspot.com)

The oldest of six children born to a restaurant chef and a seamstress, Wade enjoyed growing up in cosmopolitan Hong Kong. As a child, he was mesmerized by the images that emerged from the makeshift darkroom that his father had set up in the bathroom. The year he finished high school, the family moved to Manhattan, where Wade fell in love with his father's hobby. He won a photography scholarship to Pace University and did graduate work at Columbia, earning an MA in anthropology under Margaret Mead.

He recalls asking the famed cultural anthropologist, "What should I do with my life?" Zen-like, she responded, "It's all up to you."

At Columbia, the ethnomusicologist Alan Lomax put Wade's photography skills to work editing folk dance documentaries. While photos and film captivated Wade, graphic design paid the bills. He did logos, newsletters, advertisements, and corporate brochures, and particularly relished designing promotional materials for the Metropolitan Museum of Art, the New York Historical Society, and other cultural institutions.

Early in his career, he met and married Lorra, an art student. The couple had three boys and for 40 years lived in the same house in Pleasantville, New York. After Lorra suffered a stroke a few years ago, they moved to Vashon to be near a son and his family.

"We see a new way of life," Wade says of island living. "In New York, we were anonymous. Here we've made many friends in no time."

Wade Yip's photo of a woman in New York City's Central Park, spring 1971.

SEEK CONTENTMENT
Linda Hoffman

For three decades, Linda Hoffman taught English literature at a large suburban high school outside Chicago. On the days when the students got caught up in a poem, a story, or a legend, the classroom buzzed with excitement. They heard the beat in Beowulf, felt the horror in Macbeth, thrilled at the romance in Hemingway. "It could be heavenly," says Linda.

Bright-eyed and enthusiastic, Linda has her own story. She was nine, growing up in Franklin Park, Illinois, when her mother, a law firm secretary, revealed that "dad," an Austrian-born tool and die maker, was her adoptive father. Her natural father had died of TB when Linda was two. No wonder she didn't look or act like her two younger siblings.

Early on, her maternal grandmother introduced Linda to the library. She loved its quiet, its musty smell, and the books that became "my best friends." Inspired by Cherry Ames, Student Nurse, she enrolled in a hospital nursing program after high school. "It was a disaster," she says. "I realized I'd rather touch minds than bodies."

She dropped out to do factory jobs, including wiring transistors in an assembly line at Zenith, to earn money for college. She completed English and teaching degrees at Northern Illinois University, where she met Chuck Hoffman in a French class and married him the weekend after graduation.

The college degree got her a job in the admitting ward in the nearby Elgin Mental Hospital. But Shakespeare had not prepared her for hostile schizophrenics or the zombie-like effects of Thorazine. When their first child was a year old, Linda and Chuck headed off to rural New Hampshire. With a second pregnancy, however, the family returned to Illinois and settled in a Chicago suburb. Linda found her ideal job, teaching English at Schaumburg High School.

Linda Hoffman teaching American Literature at Schaumburg High School in suburban Chicago.

Their time in New England convinced Linda that she and Chuck should retire in "a little cottage by the sea." Their son, living in Seattle, raved about the Pacific Northwest. When retirement came, Linda and Chuck ventured west, discovered Vashon, and bought their little cottage in Gold Beach. "I've never been happier," says Linda, quoting the poet Billy Collins: "tonight, the lion of contentment has placed a warm heavy paw on my chest."

SEEK SERENITY
Richard Rogers

Serenity has been an elusive goal in Richard Rogers' life. One of five children born to an IBM engineer and a British mother, Richard grew up in Tallahassee. At age 4, he was diagnosed with polio, separated from family, and sent off to Warm Springs, Georgia, for months of treatment. His body recovered but the anxiety he internalized as a child lurked in his unconscious.

Richard immersed himself in photography—he had a Kodak Brownie as a child—and set off for college at Florida State. He fell into a job at an alternative weekly, where he took pictures of Richard Nixon, Abbie Hoffman, and the Black Panthers. The paper folded. Richard, hungry for personal peace in the midst of the Vietnam War, took up yoga and meditation. He became a disciple of Maharaji, a teenage Indian guru who taught that peace is found within. After a pilgrimage to India, Richard moved into an ashram in Tallahassee and later shared a Denver ashram with 40 Maharaji followers from 14 nations. He was asked to design publications, learned on the job, and began his graphics career.

He fell in love and married Susan, another Maharaji follower, and the two moved to urban Miami, where they continued to meditate. "It gave us a sense of calm and inner beauty amidst the chaos around us," Richard says.

In 1980 he started his own business, Rogers Graphics, designing promotional materials for tropical produce. He realized that with a phone, a fax, and FedEx, he could do business from anywhere. So, after enduring burglars, car thieves, and drug dealers in Miami, Richard and Susan discovered Vashon in 1989 and never left. Richard designed for Beall's Roses, Vashon Allied Arts, Vashon Audubon, Church of Great Rain, Drama Dock and Voice of Vashon.

He thought he had found tranquility. But the national trauma of 9/11 reawakened the childhood ghosts, plunging Richard into psychological paralysis. Therapy allowed him to release the pain and grief he had suppressed for 50 years, as did a visit to the very room where he was confined at Warm Springs. Today Richard does his design work at home in a 28-sided, tri-level yurt he designed with a soaring mandala dome. The skylit dome floods the interior with natural light and invites serenity.

Caricature of Richard Rogers drawn in 1974 by a Denver ashram friend.

SEEK UNDERSTANDING
Thomas Abraham

Thomas Abraham is an unusual man. He's lived on three islands: Bahrain, a small Arab kingdom in the Persian Gulf; Manhattan; and now Vashon. His mother tongue — Malayalam — can be spelled backward and forward. He's a writer whose Christian parents emigrated from predominantly Hindu India. And his mission has been to impart a better understanding of the Arab and Islamic world.

"Popular media often presented Arabs as backward, camel-riding ragheads," says Thomas, a slight, thoughtful fellow whose faith has guided his work.

The oldest of four boys born in Bahrain to a dentist father and a doctor mother, Thomas was sent off to boarding school in India at age five. He hated the military discipline, the separation from family, the cold hill station isolated in Tamil Nadu. But a teacher awakened him to literature. He fell in love with the romantic poets and later with the works of D.H. Lawrence. After completing a BA and MA, he went back to Bahrain to discover that teaching English to Arab kids gave him little satisfaction.

He found a translation job at a government news agency, then a job reporting for a local daily. He liked writing the news but felt so untrained that he went abroad to study journalism in the UK and the US. In 1981 he returned to Bahrain, where he met and married an American missionary. The couple had a child and moved to Manhattan so she could complete her ministerial education at Union Seminary. Thomas worked a series of Middle East-related jobs writing about and advocating for refugees, the Kurds, religious minorities, and the dispossessed. His marriage ended, but Thomas stayed in New York City until called to India in 2007 to care for his ailing parents.

When his parents passed away, Thomas had to decide where in the world to live. He fondly recalled Vashon from a chance visit. Hmmm, he thought, when he settled here in 2017, this is an island I'm choosing.

Thomas Abraham, left, draws in a cartooning class in his boarding school in Tamil Nadu, India, in the 1960s.

SERENDIPITY
Bruce Haulman

When Bruce Haulman, Vashon's resident historian, describes his life, he uses the word "serendipity," which means "good luck in finding valuable things by chance."

It was serendipity that caused Bruce, a Florida boy in a PhD program at Texas, to fall in love with a fellow student who had grown up in Burien with an enchanting view of Vashon. "On her romantic notion, we married and moved here in 1973," he says. The relationship ended but Bruce stayed on. Years later he was walking on KVI Beach when he met Pam Hamilton, a one-week summer visitor, and fell in love again. Another case of serendipity. They remain married today.

Perhaps it was serendipity that caused him to decline an invitation to join the Foreign Service, pass up a Peace Corps assignment to India, and instead pursue an unlikely career in history and film. He wrote a PhD dissertation at the University of Washington that contrasted the culture of American Westerns (male, action over words, exclusion) with that of films set in schools (feminine, feelings, inclusion).

For nearly 40 years he has taught at Green River College in Auburn. Well, not exactly. After a six-year stint as Metro Transit's budget manager, Bruce began at GRC in 1981 as an academic dean. But being the boss was less satisfying than teaching, so he took a cut in pay and power and returned to the classroom. He never regretted it.

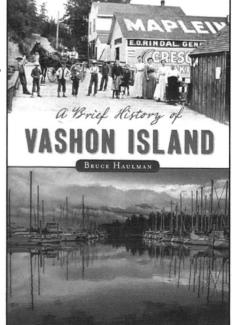

A relaxed, affable semi-retiree who clearly delights in both history and film, Bruce continues to direct GRC's January-March study program in Australia and New Zealand. "My wife complains I haven't seen a Pacific Northwest winter in 20 years," he jokes.

The author of two books on Vashon's history, Bruce helped stage the Heritage Museum's special exhibits about artists Abby Williams Hill and Marshall Sohl, the Point Robinson lighthouse, Ellisport/Chautauqua, and the Japanese presence on the island. "My main interest now," he says, "is Vashon's unique history."

Vashon resident Bruce Haulman wrote the island's history.

SERVE YOUR COMMUNITY
Lynne Ameling

For Lynne Ameling, a breakthrough moment came when a dementia patient she was caring for remembered the word that she herself could not bring to mind. The word was "request." Lynne was talking about a sign she'd seen in a historic New Orleans jazz joint advising patrons that anyone who requested "When the Saints Come Marching In" would pay a premium because the musicians were tired of playing it. And sure enough, once the word "request" was recalled and the song mentioned, the adult day program in the Vashon Lutheran Church spontaneously belted out "When the Saints Come Marching In."

Lynne, co-founder of the program, and other volunteers give regular caregivers a respite by providing art, music, and companionship to loved ones with Alzheimer's, brain injuries, and other impairments of the mind. (Visit vashoneldercare.com to volunteer.)

"The program has taught me to live in the moment," says Lynne, a retired teacher. "For that moment, we've made a person's life come alive."

Respite care is not the only program Lynne began in retirement. She also started an English as a Second Language (ESL) class at St. John Vianney Catholic Church. She quickly figured out what makes for a successful program: provide childcare and recruit high schoolers studying Spanish to do the childcare. The parents learn English undisturbed while the high school students improve their Spanish by helping Hispanic kids with homework. In fact, the Hispanic kids consider it their English class.

Born in Akron, Ohio, Lynne went to Catholic schools ("saddle shoes for 12 years") including the University of Dayton, where she met her husband Bill and married him the week after graduation. The Air Force sent them to Idaho. After Bill's discharge, they and their two toddlers moved to Seattle and, in 1976, to Vashon. Why? Because a map showed that the island was midway between his job in Seattle's Pioneer Square and her first teaching job in Gig Harbor. They built a house on the north end and have lived there ever since.

Lynne Ameling, standing right, co-founder of the respite care program at the Lutheran Church, poses with Halloween trick or treaters and adults with dementia and brain injuries.

SET GOALS
Maureen Emenegger

Early on Maureen Emenegger knew what she wanted in life: a nursing job, a good man (she's had two), and two children (she was blessed with three).

"I set my goals as a high school sophomore," says Maureen, a clever, good-humored daughter of a farm family that raised alfalfa, pigs, chickens, rabbits, and cows in rural Pend Oreille County.

A home economics nursing class convinced Maureen to become a nurse. To satisfy entry requirements, she left the farm and boarded with a teacher, first in Walla Walla, and then in Fife, where she graduated from high school in 1951. She went on to complete her nursing training at Tacoma General Hospital and leapt into the surgery department. "I loved surgery," says Maureen, who discovered she was especially dexterous at handling medical instruments.

One day she spotted John Emenegger pumping gas at the Mobil station across from the Poodle Dog Restaurant. John saw her too but was soon enlisted in the Navy. He sent a message through a neighbor boy that he'd like her to write him. She did. For four years, as the Navy shipped him back and forth to Japan, they corresponded. "He came home for my nursing graduation," Maureen recalls, "and proposed that night."

They married, built a home in Fife, had two boys and a girl. Maureen became a "stay-at-home mom," involving herself in her children's school activities. John's new job with a garden company took the family to Spokane for 17 years and then to Portland. Life was good. The couple enjoyed salmon fishing, world travel, and eight grandkids. (Grandma's advice: "Go for it.") After John died in 2005, a lonely Maureen sold their Vancouver home and moved to a mobile park.

It was there that Keith Putnam, a widower, Vashon architect, and good man No. 2, entered her life through seniormatch.com. Months of Vashon-Vancouver commuting ensued. And when Keith proposed that they live together on the island, Maureen went for it.

I set my goals as a high school sophomore.

SHARE YOUR PASSION
Char Phillips

A horse trainer, puppy raiser, and outdoorswoman, Char Phillips believes in sharing her passion for animals, especially with kids. She discovered as a child that learning to handle and care for animals gave her confidence and self-assurance.

"4-H changed my life," says Char, a patient, quiet-spoken introvert. "I came out of my shell. I was so proud that I could train a dog or a horse."

Raised in Everett, the younger child of a mill worker and a homemaker, Char saved $75 in allowance to buy her first horse at age 13. It came with a saddle, a halter, and new shoes. She graduated from Cascade High School, then completed a recreation degree at Central Washington. In the summer, she was riding master at Camp Nor'wester on Lopez Island and, in the winter, a ski instructor at Alpental. Later she moved to Lake Stevens to work for a horse trainer and soon boarded and bred horses at Centaur Ranch.

A horse connection led to a role in the 1982 western *Harry Tracy, Desperado*, in which Char, dressed in tux, tails, and mustache, drives a horse carriage. She's in the credits along with Bruce Dern, Helen Shaver, and Gordon Lightfoot. Around the same time, Char met Nelson Phillips in a tack shop in Marysville and fell in love.

Nelson persuaded her to move to Vashon, where she continued to keep horses (currently, Truffles and Gypsy) and upped her training of guide dogs for the blind. Realm, her current puppy, is the 22nd dog she has trained since 1999. At the middle and high schools, she started a guide-dog training program for students.

With a day job as school bus driver and Vashon High School athletic secretary, Char talks to lots of students about animals and the outdoors. She is club advisor for the VHS outdoor club, a board member of the Vashon Ski School, and president of the Vashon-Maury Horse Association. Dogs, horses, and kids, she says, can be great joys.

Char Phillips, 16, and Peg, the first dog she trained for Guide Dogs for the Blind, with its new master in 1967.

STAY PUT
Neil Beaumont

Neil Beaumont is proof of the old adage: There's no place like home. He lives on the Lisabeula property with the big yellow farmhouse that his grandparents bought in 1912. His dad, a night watchman for the ferries, and his mom, a homemaker, raised him and three siblings there on 30 acres given over to currants, cherries, apples, and cattle. He went to Burton Elementary (its north end rival was Vashon Elementary) and played basketball and baseball at Vashon High.

The Army drafted Neil as soon as he graduated. After basic training at Fort Ord, California, and marine engineer school at Fort Eustis, Virginia, he was assigned to a landing craft based at Qui Nhon, Vietnam. He and his fellow soldiers lived in tents on the beach and hauled ammo, guns, food, and beer from ship to shore.

There was a war going on around us but we were fairly safe.

"There was a war going on around us but we were fairly safe," says Neil, a good-humored guy who makes the best of bad situations. When his two-year Army stint was over, he returned home to Vashon for good. He was scarcely back when both his parents died at the family home on the very same day. The four kids divided the property and Neil subsequently moved an Evergreen modular home onto his share. He's lived there ever since.

For virtually all of his work career, Neil was an oiler on the ferries, mostly pulling 12-hour, seven-day shifts one week with the next week off. He did the job for 30 years. "I absolutely liked it," he says. "You're your own boss down below in the engine room."

Neil calls himself a bachelor although, in retirement, he's had a couple of partners. The first, Mary Mascolino, passed away in 2011. A year later he met Pat Douglass, a widow, at the Salton Sea, California, mobile home park where he has wintered for 20 years. "The next year I came home and she came with me," he says, beaming.

START OVER
Kate Huntley

Three times a week Kate Huntley begins the day grocery shopping for the two to three dozen people who will come to lunch at the Vashon Senior Center. It's a challenge. She never knows for sure how many will show up. At the last minute, she may need to stretch the meatloaf or supplement the chicken noodle casserole.

"But I love it," says Kate, a no-nonsense woman who collects recipes and cookbooks. "It's fun interacting with the folks who come here."

It's fun interacting with the folks who come here.

The daughter of a carpenter and a ballet teacher, Kate grew up in Boulder, Colorado, and came to cooking by starting over several times. Her first job, as a 12-year-old, was pulling cockleburs off wild horses. She was paid 50 cents a horse. She later skinned dead animals for a taxidermist and went off to college thinking she'd be a veterinarian. Instead, she became a cable splicer, climbing telephone poles in the dead of winter. She got addicted to drugs but kicked the habit by starting over in Albany, New York, as a grocery store clerk.

In 1984, at the urging of a friend, Kate moved to Vashon. She took up carpentry, doing remodels and ultimately clearing five acres and building her own house on the west side. Her building skills led to teaching carpentry to "non-traditional" (i.e., women) students at Renton Technical College. After two years, she started over again, completed a master's degree in counseling, and flew off to Alaska to serve as an "itinerant therapist" to four native villages above the Arctic Circle. It was a tough job dealing with alcoholism, suicide, and cultural loss.

Returning to Vashon in 1997, Kate was briefly a short-order cook at Sporty's before working as a staff member at two psychiatric hospitals in Seattle. Eventually she became a case manager at Seattle Mental Health, where her clients were mentally ill offenders just out of prison. Like her, they were starting over again.

STEP UP AND DO SOMETHING
Sue Weston

It would be a rare day when Sue Weston, an energetic, rosy-cheeked go-getter, had nothing to do. At the Senior Center, she builds birdhouses, does knitting and needlepoint, and enjoys the noontime lunch. She volunteers at Vashon Community Care, serves as a deacon at the Presbyterian Church, and makes macaroni salads for the Vashon Community Meal. And, as a member of the county Advisory Council on Aging and Disability Services, she advocates for the elderly and disabled.

Describing herself as "an unconventional Christian," Sue says, "I believe we are here to help, to step up and do what we can."

A fourth-generation Vashonite, Sue lives in the Sylvan Beach home that her great-grandparents first erected as a platform tent in 1907. It's where she returned after a nomadic 16-year-marriage to a high school music director took her to small towns throughout the state and Canada and left her with two daughters. "I had a very restless husband," she says.

Sue Weston, playing Sweet Flossie Farmer, sings with a snake in Drama Dock's 1986 show, "A Slice of Vashon."

Sue promised her girls they would stay put on Vashon. "I wanted rootedness." Four decades later, she's been here long enough to do two Drama Dock productions of the *Pirates of Penzance.* She played a maiden the first time, the governess the second. For some years, she commuted off-island to study drafting at South Seattle College and library science at Highline College, and then earn a degree at the University of Washington Tacoma. The BA got her a job as a research librarian, but Sue, ever practical, discovered she could make better money photocopying.

Eventually, she got an on-island job at the *Beachcomber,* which, in those days, also sold art and offices supplies. After the paper sold in 1995, Sue worked as a church secretary and a hostess at the Backbay Inn. But her last job, caring for her dying mother, touched her most deeply. "Caregiving," she says, "is so demanding and so undervalued."

TAKE RISKS
Trudy Rosemarin

Trudy Rosemarin figures she escaped a boring, conventional life in her native Basel, Switzerland because she took risks. It was not an approach that pleased her strait-laced parents.

At the Maedchen Gymnasium, a public school for bright girls, Trudy immersed herself in languages: English, French, Italian, and German. At 16, with earnings from a summer job as a nurse's aide, she paid her own way for a three-week student exchange to the UK. London blew her mind. The freedom, the excitement, the diversity. "It changed me forever," she says.

Trudy finished school in Basel and set off for London again as an au pair and later found an au pair job in California. But taking care of wealthy families' kids was not getting her anywhere. In Palo Alto, she answered an advertisement to work in the foreign government document division at Stanford's Hoover Library. She flunked the typing test, but her multi-lingual ability got her the job. "I am a very determined person," says Trudy, who has climbed every volcanic peak in the state.

In 1969 she met her first husband, a computer systems analyst, at a church volleyball game. She moved back to Switzerland when he got a job in Basel. They had two kids but soon wanted to be back in the States. When Boeing offered him a job in Seattle, they bought a house on Vashon. With the kids in school, Trudy marketed her language skills. She directed the Inlingua School at Southcenter, lining up teachers for private instruction in everything from Russian to Urdu. "It was like running my own little UN," she says.

But the pay was so-so, and she was now divorced. For 19 years she managed the Seattle office of a press-clipping bureau, where the autonomy was great but keeping up with the news was stressful. She wanted her own business.

In 1991 Trudy and second husband Chaim Rosemarin moved to a five-acre island property, where she began growing masses of flowers. She sold them at the Saturday market, made floral arrangements for weddings, and, in 1998, took a big risk by leasing space in Seattle's 2nd & Seneca Building. She opened Trudy's Floral Design. It was successful and immensely satisfying. "Working with that incredible floral beauty," she says, "I made people happy all day long."

TALK LESS, LISTEN MORE
Marlys Svensson

For a woman who participates in three book clubs, you might think that Marlys Svensson would talk a lot. You'd be wrong. Marlys prefers to listen. "I like to listen and learn from others," says Marlys, who has spent a lifetime learning through an unusual childhood and a 58-year-marriage to a Norwegian immigrant.

Born to German-American parents in Cut Bank, Montana, Marlys spent her early years in a boxcar that traveled the Great Northern rail line as her father supervised gandy dancers laying track. Her mother cooked for the work crew. Marlys was schooled in northern Idaho, where she was valedictorian at Bonner's Ferry High School. It was an innocent time. One day the whole school was grounded after a student stole two pens from the post office.

Marlys won a scholarship to Valparaiso, a Lutheran college in Indiana, but found the Midwestern culture too stiff and confining. She transferred to the University of Washington, where she studied education and lived in a boarding house behind the Blue Moon Tavern. Rather than frequent the tavern, she joined the Skandia Folkdance Society, where she met Einar Svensson, a structural engineer and international cross-country skier. They married and found work. She taught fifth grade and he helped design Seattle's Monorail.

It was an adventurous partnership. Marlys accompanied Einar to Norway, where he worked on an oil platform, she learned Norwegian, and they had the first of their two children. Returning to Seattle, they started a business called "Haida-Hide," manufacturing and selling prefabricated cedar homes. Eventually they built a cedar chalet near Snoqualmie Pass, where they lived when not skiing elsewhere.

In 2013 fire destroyed the chalet and their most precious possessions: photos, paintings, books, Einar's engineering designs… "The fire gave me a different outlook on life," Marlys says. "Value is not in stuff; it's in memories." Homeless, they moved to their son's house in Burton, where they live today.

Marlys Svensson, 4, clutches a stuffed bunny outside the Great Northern housing cars where she lived with her parents and 40 gandy dancers.

TEACH, LEARN, EAT LOCAL
Merrilee Runyan

Merrilee Runyan has been a grade school teacher, a Weyerhaeuser manager, a lavender grower, and a community organizer whose efforts helped create Sustainable Vashon and an innovative program run by the Vashon Island Growers Association (VIGA). The Food Access Partnership invented a new currency: VIGA Bucks. Its subsidized coupons help food stamp recipients buy fresh fruits and vegetables at the Saturday Market and at island farm stands.

"We want to make local food available to all while providing a livable income for island farmers," explains Merrilee, a cheery, energetic retiree. She and two partners once ran the Lavender Sisters Farm, which supplied thousands of lavender bunches to area florists. "There was a time," she laughs, "when lavender was a hot thing."

At Sustainable Vashon, Merrilee is on a six-member council that encourages viable solutions for Vashon problems. For example, the group sponsored a solar demonstration project with Puget Sound Energy and addressed racism by encouraging islanders to read and discuss the book *Waking Up White*.

The older of two girls born to a Stanford administrator and a San Jose State speech professor, Merrilee grew up in Palo Alto, California, on a path to be a teacher. She earned a history degree at Stanford and a master's degree in education at Claremont. Her first charges were "behaviorally challenged" kids in Newport Beach, California. In 1974, she and her family moved north, determined to live somewhere on Puget Sound. She taught preschool at Bates Technical and Green River Colleges, directed the child care program at Tacoma Community College, spent 18 months at the University of Puget Sound Law School, and landed at Weyerhaeuser as manager of equal opportunity employment.

But Merrilee missed teaching. She returned to the classroom, taking tough jobs at inner-city schools in Tacoma. "I'm passionate around issues of fairness and equity," she says, "and I love seeing kids realize they can learn." One of her retirement avocations is learning how and why other cultures value the elderly more than we do. And what we can do about it.

I'm passionate around issues of fairness and equity.

TEAMWORK
Linda Peterson

For Linda Peterson, life's most fulfilling times involved teamwork: On an archaeological dig in Israel, where she lived in a kibbutz. At a cerebral palsy school in New Jersey, where she gave her Scout troop personalized merit badges for mastering their leg braces and wheelchairs. At the Washington State Cerebral Palsy Center in Shoreline, where she was a member of a diagnostic team that designed individual learning plans for the school's residents.

"The best jobs in my life," says Linda, who retired as a special ed teacher on Vashon, "were on teams. Working together, we created a future for students."

One of four children born to a chemical engineer and a homemaker, she grew up with goats, a cow, and chickens on five acres in Portland, Oregon. The family had a big vegetable garden and viewed white sugar and white flour as poison. "We ate brown," Linda says. She attended a Catholic grade school and all-girls Marycrest High School and biked home for lunch.

Without teamwork, Linda's life could have gone differently. She's dyslexic. School was challenging. A friend got her through chemistry. And while Linda washed the dishes, her mother read her Dickens' *A Tale of Two Cities*. Twice. Linda graduated and, miraculously, the nearby University of Portland accepted her. Three and a half years later, she had a BA in elementary education and a substitute teaching job.

But Europe beckoned. Linda and two friends took the Greyhound across the country, then a Danish coal freighter to Germany, and began hitchhiking. Six months later, Linda was sewing lace slips in a Paris sweatshop for 50 cents an hour. She asked her mom to send her a winter coat.

Once back home, she completed a master's in special ed and taught in Oregon, California, New Jersey and, eventually, as "institution teacher" at the state cerebral palsy center. One day at the Seattle Center fountain, an Army National Guard member on weekend leave approached her and said, "Are you waiting for anyone else?" "No," Linda replied. She and Gary Peterson went on a first date that night—to the Ringling Brothers Circus. They'll soon celebrate their golden jubilee.

Linda Peterson, then "Miss Thwaite," poses with her students in this 1966 photo at a state cerebral palsy school in Belleville, New Jersey.

THINK FREELY
Mary Robinson

You wouldn't guess that Mary Robinson, who started kindergarten on the French Riviera and finished high school at an exclusive, all-girls Catholic boarding school outside Boston, would become a "free-thinking rebel." But those same nuns who primed her for sophisticated cocktail chatter also taught her to think, speak, and write critically. "They were wonderful," she says. "I learned so much."

By the time Mary, the oldest of six kids raised by a US Navy captain and a homemaker, graduated from Syracuse University with a degree in comparative religion, she was enamored with the counterculture. She participated in teach-ins on racism, the freedom riders, the Vietnam War. She and a girlfriend, with whom she still travels today, hitchhiked around Europe, confident in "our faith to get out of any situation." There were several.

After college, Mary and a boyfriend drove west, arriving in Seattle on a clear, iridescent January day. The boyfriend left, but she stayed. She earned a teaching degree at the University of Washington, where she fell in love with a botanist. She followed him to Hawaii and they married. Returning to the Northwest, the botanist began a landscape business, and Mary began working in clay: statuettes, animals, and figurines influenced by a growing interest in antiquities. Her ceramic art sold

well enough to support sojourns to Mexico and Central America and later to the Middle East. "Those cultures taught me about living," she says.

Mary's marriage to the botanist ended when he fully recognized he was gay. Yet their relationship endured. She tended the five acres he purchased on Vashon and, when he was dying of AIDs, she cared for him until the end. The property, with its vintage house, pond, and gardens, became hers. She uses it well, growing flowers for a Madison Park florist, teaching horticulture to students, and hosting the neighborhood summer party.

She marvels at the beauty around her. Gazing at backyard firs soaring into a vast blue sky, Mary says, "I guess I've become an animist. Look how those trees connect the earth to the sky."

Mary Robinson at a truck stop, which included a prayer room, dining hall and farmers' market, in southern Iran in 2020.

TRAVEL OPENS EYES
Edna Dam

Edna Dam was a teenager just off her parents' dairy farm and doing a dull office job in Vancouver, BC, when Marlene, a co-worker, said one day, "Let's travel the world."

So in the fall of 1957, they bought plane tickets to Boise — their first experience of air travel and the farthest destination they could afford — and began a year and a half of traveling punctuated by periods of work. They took the Greyhound to Dallas, Mobile, and Charleston. Then up the East Coast to Baltimore, Boston, and Philadelphia. They spent a winter in Montreal, doing temp jobs, then sailed on a Cunard ship to London, working some more and lodging at the Overseas Visitors Club. Then it was on to Geneva for temp jobs with a UN agency. They bought a motor scooter and, Roman Holiday-style, rode all over southern Europe until the Lambretta went kaput in Yugoslavia.

A thoughtful, unassuming woman who eventually completed degrees in teaching and comparative literature, Edna did copy editing at Boeing and technical writing for a phone equipment company, but it's her travels that make her smile. She and Jim Dam, her husband of 66 years, were near-newlyweds when they bought a Volvo in Sweden to tour Europe together.

"I loved travel and study," Edna says, "but I never got much satisfaction from anything someone would pay me to do."

In fact, Edna quit one Boeing job because there was nothing to do. At age 53 she retired, which, she says, is much more fun. She and Jim sold their Seattle home and in 1997 built a new one in the woods on Vashon. Edna joined the Garden Club, the Quaker Fellowship, and the Vashon Chorale.

She loves her life and feels grateful for good health, a long marriage, and the island community. And she still stays in touch with Marlene, who launched her youthful odyssey all those years ago.

Marlene Stevenson and Edna Dam, center, in helmets and sunglasses,
got their motor scooter running again thanks to these Sicilian villagers.

TRUST A FRIEND
Sara Van Fleet

On at least three occasions the willingness of Sara Van Fleet to trust a friend's advice turned her life around. The only daughter of a Kimberly-Clark executive and a homemaker, Sara spent six childhood years with her family in Sydney, Australia. She returned to her native Wisconsin with a thick accent, dated clothes, and the feeling of an outsider. But at an unlikely private college in Ohio she discovered the 'Homestead,' an off-the-grid, self-governing, residential campus farm. The student farmers had no electricity, a big garden, a curriculum to plan, and a goat to milk. Sara bunked with Betsy, another misfit.

Years later Sara was in Seattle preparing for grad school when Betsy phoned her out of the blue. "Sara," she said, "there's a guy in Seattle you've got to meet. You are like two peas in a pod." Betsy provided phone numbers but nothing happened. Finally, Sara called. Sam invited her to a homemade dinner, and they've been together ever since—32 years.

Sara had plans to be a lawyer until Kelly, her best friend in high school, invited her to a remote Philippine island. She traveled there by jet, prop plane, jeep, and canoe, met up with Kelly, stayed three months, and fell in love with Southeast Asia. Forget law school. Sara would be an anthropologist.

Sara Van Fleet, right, and Claudine Kim-Murphy are fellow Zumba instructors on Vashon and trusted friends.

She enrolled at the University of Washington, where she was mentored by the professor who founded the SE Asia Studies Center. "Besides Sam," Sara says, "it was the best thing that ever happened to me." For the next 10 years, two of them on a Fulbright in Chiang Mai, Thailand, Sara worked on her PhD. Her dissertation was titled "Everyday Dramas: Television and Modern Thai Women." When she finished, she and Sam moved to Vashon, and the SE Asia Studies Center named her its managing director.

Her friend Dari, who had started Zumba on the island, convinced Sara to become a dance music instructor. "Trust me," Dari said. Sara did. She calls her decision "transformative" and now teaches Zumba and plays bass guitar in a band. My, what friends can do!

TRY NEW THINGS
Molly Green

Molly Green was contentedly studying at Whitman College when her single mother pulled her and her two sisters out of school, sold their beautiful home on Seattle's Capitol Hill, booked passage for the family on a boat to Rotterdam, and embarked on an 18-month jaunt around Europe in a red Volvo. This grand adventure included hosteling, occasionally sleeping in the car, living in a Swiss chalet at the uphill end of a funicular, and, in Molly's case, a French immersion course with 20 Saudi boys.

The trip not only gave Molly a crash course in cultural awareness, it opened her eyes to the possibilities of fiber art. Once back home, she forsook Whitman and earned an art degree at the UW. For the oldest daughter of a pathologist and a grade school teacher, art was not an obvious pursuit. A good student, Molly had been a cheerleader at Lincoln High School, where she graduated in a class of 700.

She married a UW architecture grad, and the two drove the Alcan Highway in January to Anchorage, where a job awaited. Molly, who prefers calling herself "a maker" rather than an artist, got to work making things. Over the years, she has made tapestries, rugs, and toddler dresses. She did private commissions and won several design competitions, including two in Tacoma to create custom street banners.

In Alaska she participated in the re-election campaign of US Sen. Ernest Gruening, one of only two senators to vote against bombing North Vietnam. He lost but Molly's peace activism continued. Returning to Seattle, she and her husband bought a house in Madrona and raised their two sons. She marched against US involvement in wars in Central America and co-founded a sister parish exchange with one in El Salvador.

For a decade, she was a congressional assistant to US Rep. Jim McDermott, focusing on visa and immigration issues. "I met people from everywhere and heard amazing stories." Her 25-year marriage ended. After some time, she happily renewed an acquaintance with Hal Green, whom she knew through a peace project in the USSR. They married in 2002 and moved to his Vashon farm, where they transformed a century-old house, planted a big garden, and turned a chicken coop into a cozy bed and breakfast.

Aside from tapestries, rugs and street banners, Molly Green makes dresses for toddlers.

UNLOCK THE TRAUMA
Joe Okimoto

When Joe Okimoto saw the pictures of children caged at the US border and agents using whips on Haitian migrants, it outraged him. He was three when soldiers arrested his family at their San Diego home and put them in a converted horse stable, where his mother gave birth to a fourth child. Two weeks later they were in a concentration camp in the Arizona desert with 18,000 other imprisoned Japanese-Americans.

"The emotional memories are stored in my body," says Joe, his eyes wet, his speech soft. "Trauma has been the center of my life without me realizing it."

His parents came to the US from Japan in 1937 as Protestant missionaries to Japanese immigrants in San Diego. After the war, they resumed pastoring. They felt so much shame, Joe says, that they did not talk about their incarceration. Joe went to Pasadena High School, where he studied hard, co-captained the football team, and was president of the Lettermen's Club.

His mother's death of cancer convinced him to go to medical school, first at Dartmouth, then Harvard, with an internship at Harborview Hospital in Seattle. He joined the Air Force as a flight surgeon, married, had two sons, and did a residency in surgery at UC San Francisco. Anti-war activists and Black Panthers were marching in the streets. "It was a major turning point for me," Joe says, "I became aware of racism and that I was one of its victims."

He began a PhD at the UW School of Public Health but dropped out to join the civil rights movement. Divorced, he met and married a fellow activist. The governor named him to the Commission on Asian Affairs; King County hired him as medical director of its drug addiction program; and, after the UW certified him in psychiatry, he was medical director of a counseling program for Asian war refugees. Later he set up his own psychiatry practice.

Yet, only late in life did Joe identify the pain in his soul: childhood trauma "caused by my government." Retired on Vashon, he facilitates a healing circle for Japanese concentration camp survivors. And he speaks out for caged children, jailed migrants, and victims of racism. Why? "Because nobody spoke up for us."

*Joe Okimoto, far left in back row, with his first grade class in 1944-45
at the Poston concentration camp in Arizona.*

USE A PERSONAL TOUCH
Marge Lofstrom

Marge Lofstrom was not expecting the doctor's response. When he surmised that her one-year-old son had valley fever, a rare life-threatening fungus, he told her, "I need to see you today." But she was in Radium Springs, New Mexico. The doctor, a specialist, was at a children's hospital in Tucson, 350 miles away. Marge got in the family's only car and drove her boy across two states. Her husband, delayed, had to hitchhike. The doctor saw them immediately, examined their son, explained the disease, and put him on six months of chemotherapy. The boy recovered completely.

"That doctor," says Marge, tearing up, "knew people in crisis need a personal touch."

That personal touch is something Marge has tried to emulate over a career centered on helping people. She's been a day care worker, a house parent to troubled girls, a bookstore clerk, a special ed teacher, and a high school vice principal. "I want to do what's right by kids," she says, "and honor their uniqueness."

The older child of an IBM electrical engineer and a homemaker, Marge grew up "a shy ordinary kid" in Poughkeepsie, New York. She majored in philosophy at Cedarcrest College, a girls school in Allentown, Pennsylvania. She met her future husband Don, a frat boy at a college nearby, on a blind date. They've been married 50 years.

After graduation, Marge and Don headed to New Mexico to start a new life. They embraced the desert, lived in an adobe house, and built a geodesic dome. Don's managerial job soon took them all over the country. At one point, the frequent moves had them paying mortgages on two houses and renting a third.

Marge Lofstrom and husband Don built a geodesic dome home in New Mexico.

Along the way Marge had a second son, taught children with learning disabilities, and completed graduate degrees in special ed and education administration. Eventually, they settled in Nashville. Her last job, before she and Don retired to Vashon in 2016 to be near their sons, was teaching gifted kids.

WALK AND REFLECT
Phil Volker

In 2013 Phil Volker was diagnosed with Stage IV colon cancer and began chemotherapy treatment. He also started walking. On the 10-acre westside property he shares with his wife, Rebecca Graves, he created a trail that starts near his front door and meanders through pasture and forest. Do it 909 times and you've covered the distance of El Camino de Santiago, the pilgrim trail across Spain that Phil walked in 2014.

Walking, whether at home or in Spain, is what Phil calls "meditative therapy." He sees his incurable cancer as a "catalyst for healing and change." He regards it as pointing the way to things he hadn't noticed or paid enough attention to before.

"I started concentrating on things that get us closer to God and fellow man," says Phil, a calm, thoughtful fellow with a ruddy complexion and a ready smile. He became a Catholic, joined St. John Vianney Parish, and invited friends and strangers alike to walk with him.

An only child born and raised in Buffalo, New York, Phil started college at Syracuse University but dropped out to enlist in the Marines, who kept him in communications at Camp Lejeune, North Carolina, rather than shipping him to Vietnam. After his three-year hitch, he drifted west, and, by happenchance, found himself stranded in a snowstorm on Vashon. He never left. He met and married Rebecca, bought the westside property, and had two children. For 40 years he labored as a carpenter and woodworker.

Now he walks, reflects, and shares his experience of cancer. He's the subject of a film, *Phil's Camino*. He speaks to people living with cancer. He writes a blog (caminoheads.com). And he invites those who walk with him to leave a small stone, a symbol of their burdens or their prayers, on the rockpile at his trailhead. As for the inevitable? "I'm not anxious," Phil says. "I'm being led to a place of peace with death."

Phil Volker walks his "camino," a trail he created through his wooded acreage.

WELCOME CHANGE
Pat Douglass

Pat Douglass marvels when she thinks back over her 30-year career at the now defunct United Telephone Company. At various times a secretary, clerk, customer service rep, truck driver, and white pages editor, Pat started with a manual Royal typewriter in 1962. She retired with a state-of-the-art computer with four screens.

"It was a great time to be in the communications business," she says. "Who would have thought we'd go from a hard-wired phone line to wireless signals?" She loved it. "I have never, ever not liked change."

I have never, ever
not liked change.

Change was not always marvelous in Pat's life. Born in Paola, Kansas, she and her younger sister were toddlers when the family moved to the Washington coast. World War II was on and Dad was in the Navy. Her parents' marriage didn't survive the war. At age three, Pat and her sister were back in Kansas living with grandma. It was tough. Despite good grades at school, Pat dropped out and married at 17. "It was the worst mistake of my life," she says. "I wasn't even pregnant."

But she soon was. She gave birth to a son who at six months was hospitalized with pneumonia. He recovered, and two accommodating principals helped her return to school and graduate. She later had a daughter, but the marriage eventually ended in divorce. In 1979 Pat wed Dale Douglass, a Kansas farm kid who became an auctioneer and realtor. Their happy home in Garnett, Kansas, lasted until his death in 2011.

In Garnett, Pat worked for the phone company, clerked auctions for Dale, served on the senior center board, and was president of the Methodist women's association. She would have continued an active work and community life but for the stroke that forced her retirement.

"God is in charge," Pat says. "You can't know joy if you've never known hurt." Joyfully, a year after meeting Neil Beaumont at a California mobile park, she agreed to move in with him on Vashon. "Change happens," she concludes. "Welcome it."

WORK CAN BE SATISFYING
John Burggraff

John Burggraff describes himself as a "nuts and bolts guy." There's nothing he enjoys more than working with hand and power tools on home improvement projects. Or, as he did for 30 years, puzzling out where to put utilities in buildings on the University of Washington campus. In fact, he's crawled through miles of underground tunnels that contain the university's electrical, steam, water, cooling, communication cables, and compressed air lines.

"Facilities is my thing," John says. His enthusiasm for construction continued after he retired from the UW in 1997. He and two buddies did what they called "widow & divorcee work" by helping single women with carpentry, plumbing, and electrical projects. The women paid for the materials and the men donated their labor.

"It was an opportunity for us guys to get together and feel good about doing something," says John, a tall, thin man with a hearty laugh.

Born in Sioux Falls, South Dakota, John was eight when his father traded farming for a job in a parts warehouse in town. John had 12 years of Catholic education so memorable that he still attends his high school reunion every five years. In 1958 he graduated from South Dakota Tech with a degree in mechanical engineering. Boeing brought him to Seattle to work on missiles. "But I got bored," he recalls. "Not enough to do."

Eventually he landed the job overseeing utility design and construction at the UW. Along the way, he married and had four boys. The marriage ended, the boys grew up, and he now has five grandkids.

In the early 1990s, John moved to Vashon to be with Janet Quimby, now his wife of 30 years, and built their home. He joined St. John Vianney Church, where he ushers, tends to the lawnmowers, and cuts firewood to help heat low-income homes. And he serves on the board of the Senior Center, where he supervised the recent building renovation. Facilities is indeed his thing.

John Burggraff, right, and other members of the wood crew at St. John Vianney Church cut firewood to help heat low-income homes.

WORK HARD
Dave Schweinler

Dave Schweinler, who practiced law in Tacoma for 50 years, chuckles recalling the case of the condo owners who refused to pay his client, the carpet layer. The owners stubbornly demanded the case go to court. After a six-day trial, the judge awarded the carpet man all he was seeking and more, and required the owners to pay all attorney fees. They appealed the decision but lost again. "I was proud of that one," Dave says.

I was proud of that one.

Dave, a lifelong athlete with a wry smile, is proud of a few things: a 62-year marriage to Mimi, 30 years' service in the Air Force, and nine marathons after age 50, including Boston. Raised on Tacoma's Hilltop, the youngest son of a bank cashier and a homemaker, Dave always worked. He stacked groceries, delivered newspapers, sold men's clothing. He met a pawnbroker who didn't want what Dave had to sell but said "I like the way you talk" and employed him.

Dave graduated from Stadium High, completed a BA at the University of Puget Sound, and earned a law degree at the University of Washington. He married Mimi three days after taking the bar exam and was commissioned as an Air Force lawyer. "That was our honeymoon," he says. First to March AFB in California and then to a SAC base in the UK. He prosecuted and defended airmen who ran afoul of the law.

Discharged in 1960, Dave and Mimi were back in Tacoma with two children and no work. Dave hung out his shingle in space he shared with two other attorneys. He had the back room next to the toilet. Those first three months, he earned $105. But hard work paid off. He eventually formed a downtown law firm with Larry Ross and grew a subsequent firm to seven lawyers. He represented a bank and did real estate, family law, and probate. And the occasional litigation over carpeting.

For 35 years, Dave and Mimi have lived on Vashon, yet every Sunday they attend Zion Lutheran Church in Tacoma, where they've been members since 1956.

WORK TOGETHER AND THINGS HAPPEN
Leslie Perry

When the Highline School District faced a tough situation, Leslie Perry was the principal to resolve it. Over her 20+ years with the district, she served as principal at five schools and was called out of retirement to rescue five more.

Take Hazel View Elementary in Burien, a diverse, immigrant, low-income school where students weren't showing up. The teachers were at wits' end. Leslie won their allegiance and secured a Kellogg grant to establish an after-school program in a nearby apartment complex that was home to a quarter of the students. They held PTA meetings there. They encouraged police to be a regular presence. They persuaded businesses to donate computers. Students reappeared and parents completed their GEDs. Hazel View won a Golden Apple Award for educational excellence. Leslie credits the school's success to people working together.

She did it again on Vashon after her husband, Steve, was diagnosed with Alzheimer's. (He died in 2018.) Recognizing that caregivers needed relief, Leslie organized an Elder Care program at the Lutheran Church. Thirty-three volunteers gave a day a week caring for adults with dementia and brain injuries so regular caregivers could have a break. The volunteers created a lively community of crafts, song, and even dance.

From the minute I saw him, I was gone.

Leslie attributes her organizational skills to her parents, who overcame tragic childhoods of abandonment and alcoholism to earn teaching degrees and provide a "fabulous upbringing" for their three children. An exemplary student, Leslie attended Catholic school in Lakewood and graduated from Aquinas Academy in Tacoma, where her classmates voted her "Miss Aquinas." At the UW, she pledged a sorority, majored in education, and, at a party, met Steve. "From the minute I saw him, I was gone," she said. "He was tall, gorgeous, and sweet."

After they married in 1969, Steve's job as a food scientist took them and, eventually, their two sons to Quincy, Washington; Albany, Oregon; and back to Seattle. In 1977 they moved to Vashon, where Leslie's maternal grandparents had homesteaded. She became the school district's speech and hearing therapist, then special education coordinator for 15 Highline schools, and finally Highline's go-to principal.

WRITE
Jeanie Okimoto

The first writing venture ended poorly. Jeanie Okimoto and her best friend, both 11, wrote and distributed a neighborhood newspaper in Shaker Heights, Ohio. A lead story noted the unusual hair color of one of the neighbors. The headline read: Mrs. Greenbaum Lit Up the Neighborhood. Mrs. Greenbaum was not amused. Jeanie's mother shut down the paper.

But Jeanie's love of storytelling only grew. Over a lifetime, she has written and published short stories, plays, and 23 books of fiction and nonfiction for both adults and children. Her books have been translated into eight languages, including Chinese and Turkish. She's won numerous book awards and appeared on Oprah, CNN, and Good Morning America.

Curious and observant, Jeanie grew up the middle child of a homemaker mom who played piano and a business executive dad who was "heavy-handed in a charming way." Jeanie was fascinated with people and flourished socially. Dad insisted she go to Depauw, a Methodist college with "no drinking and no cars." At 18, she married an Air Force ROTC student. After his graduation and assignment, the couple lived on three US airbases over five years and had two daughters.

The marriage foundered. But it led to Jeanie's first book, *My Mother is Not Married to My Father*, which explains divorce to children with both humor and hope. Through her involvement in the civil rights movement, Jeanie met Joe Okimoto, a divorced

father with two boys. After they married, she wrote a sequel about second marriages and step-siblings. She enrolled at the University of Washington, where she observed child therapy sessions, and completed an MA in psychology at Antioch University. She opened a counseling practice near Children's Hospital in Seattle while continuing to write stories. For 30 years she chaired an annual program to recognize Seattle fifth graders who made the most improvement in reading. "Something I loved as much as anything I've ever done," she says.

After Jeanie and Joe moved to Vashon in 2004, she retired from counseling, concentrated on writing adult novels, and founded Endicott and Hugh Books, a small publishing house that has printed local authors and poets. Jeanie, with a notepad at hand, says, "Writing feeds my life."

Former Mayor Norm Rice and Jeanie Okimoto present certificates to students at the Seattle Reading Awards.

SENIORS OF VASHON ISLAND

A

Abraham, Thomas . 126

Ameling, Lynne . . 128

Aguilar, Lydia 51

B

Bauer, Dorothy 97

Beaumont, Neil. . . 132

Beardsley, Marge. . . 46

Becker, Jay 68

Bennington, Zoe . . . 33

Benowitz, Steve . . . 98

Beymer, Betty. . . . 54

Bloch, Alice 109

Brown, Brian 39

Brown, Jim 69

Bryan, Joe 48

Bryce, Bill 57

Butler, Carol 30

Burggraff, John . . . 151

Burnham, Greg. . . . 95

C

Campbell, Tink 32

Carney, Tim. 81

Caulton, Donna . . . 63

Christianson, Raynor . 66

Clabaugh, Ted 11

Cole, David 104

Craighead, Tom . . . 65

Coldeen, Carl 25

D

Dam, Edna 142

Dam, Jim 79

Dean, Lawrence . . . 88

Dinsmore, June 64

Dinsmore, Tom. . . 114

Douglass, Pat 150

Dunn, John 117

E

Eber, Deena 15

Emenegger, Maureen . 130

Estes, Lorna 113

Eustice, George 77

F

Fletcher, Wally 19

Franklin, Dick 55

G

Gaul, Scott 107

Grace, Midge 92

Green, Hal 83

Green, Molly 145

Grist, Penny 36

Gustafson, Barb . . . 41

H

Hallowell, Bob . . . 115

Haulman, Bruce . . 127

Hawkins, Betty 43

Hawkins, Bob. 31

Hoffman, Chuck 9

Hoffman, Linda . . 124

Hofman, Lindsay. . . 20

Huntley, Kate. . . . 133

I

Irish, Ann 119

J

Jungemann, Neil . . 101

K

Kalhorn, Susie . . . 105

Kimmel, Penny 82

Klob, Marilyn. 74

Kritzman, Ellen 96

L

Langland, June . . . 110

Lakey, Julia 76

Lindgren, Elise 59

Lodahl, Luella 38

Lofstrom, Don 29

Lofstrom, Marge . . 148

M

Malone, Sean 72

Masi, Charlotte . . . 108

McMahan, Pam. . . . 58

Moore, John. 24

N

Nagler, Mary Anne. 112

Nagler, Richard . . . 34

Nelson, Harriet. . . . 14

Nelson, Rich 56

O

Okimoto, Jeanie . . 155

Okimoto, Joe 146

O'Donnell, Michael . 67

O'Malley, Bernie . . . 49

P

Pekarek, Mary . . . 106

Perry, Jan 47

Perry, Leslie. 154

Peterson, Gary 44

Peterson, Geri 42

Peterson, Linda. . . 139

Phillips, Char 131

Prior, Keith 62

Purpus, Daphne . . . 27

Putnam, Keith 84

Q

Quenneville, Mike . . 78

R

Radford, Nancy . . . 61

Roberts, Tanya 12

Robinson, Mary . . 141

Rogers, Dave 91

Rogers, Richard . . 125

Rogers, Susan. 70

Rosemarin, Chaim . . 86

Rosemarin, Trudy . 135

Runyan, Merrilee. . 138

S

Schlumpf, Jake 89

Schweinler, Dave. . 153

Sheehan, Rain 26

Sikorski, Carrie. . . 118

Skeffington, Bev . . . 60

Skeffington, Jacq . . . 99

Slaughter, Al 45

Slaughter, Carol . . . 85

Smith, Kate 102

Spangler, Bob. 22

Spangler, Carol. . . . 90

Sparkes, Reva. 28

Stone, CC 94

Stoddard, Barb 53

Strandberg, Annie . . 71

Strandberg, Lars . . . 23

Svensson, Marlys. . 136

Swartz, Bill 116

T

Thomas, Sigrid 8

Trout, Ellen 52

Tuel, Mary 10

Tuma, Doug 87

Tuttle, Anne 17

V

Vanderpool, Nancy . 121

Vanderpool, Dick . . 16

Van Fleet, Sara . . . 144

Volker, Phil 149

W

Walker, Lornie . . . 103

Watney, Jack 75

Weston, Sue. 134

Wharton, Wendy. . . 80

White, Beth 93

Y

Yip, Wade. 122

ACKNOWLEDGMENTS

I am especially grateful to the Vashon Island seniors willing to talk with me about their lives and help me draw a lesson from what they had learned.

By my count, nine seniors profiled in the book have passed away since the first "Life Lesson" appeared in the *Beachcomber* on June 28, 2017. May they rest in eternal peace. Among the lessons they left behind are: Live boldly, Expect the unexpected, and Delight in people.

Life Lessons would not have happened without the help and encouragement of the staff and members of Vashon-Maury Senior Center. I am particularly indebted to Catherine Swearingen, executive director; Kathleen Hendrickson, operations manager and receptionist; and Mary Ornstead, business manager. Kathleen, who knew virtually everyone who walked in the door, was especially helpful in identifying likely interviewees. I want to recognize Susie Kalhorn, the energetic, creative Board president who suggested to me, a fellow Board member at the time, the idea of writing senior profiles for the *Beachcomber*. And I want to thank Mona Hardy, who did a couple of initial interviews, but succumbed to cancer as we got underway.

Daralyn Anderson, the *Beachcomber* publisher, not only welcomed the idea but found advertising support to help carry it out. Liz Shepherd, the editor, gave us permission to republish *Beachcomber* photos. The paper's publication of Life Lessons has been sponsored by Bill and LeeAnn Brown, of the Brown Insurance Agency, and later by Beth de Groen, of Windermere Real Estate.

From day one, Mike Masi, a graphic designer and a senior, has worked pro bono to design the column, enhance the photos, and make the copy fit.

Nonetheless, Mike was pleased to have Richard Rogers, a graphic design colleague and a senior, take on the book design project. Richard proved equally adept at laying out pages and reviving the faded and soiled pictures of yesteryear.

Alice Bloch, a writer and editor (and another senior), joined Richard and me to edit the book. She read and reread the copy for grammar, punctuation, and overall sense. She checked facts, noted repetition, and ensured coherent writing.

Richard, Alice and I are delighted to tell the stories, present the photos, and share the lessons of these seniors.

John A. McCoy

ABOUT THE AUTHOR

John A. McCoy is a Vashon Island senior. He is an author, journalism teacher, book club convenor, church lector, and Cub Scout den leader. He also manages the chickens at Aeggy's Farm, where he and his wife, Karen, live and raised their three children.

ABOUT THE DESIGNER

Richard Rogers is a graphic designer, avid photographer, author of *100 Words for Rain - A Whimsical Weather Guide to Pacific Northwest Precipitation* and manages the website and marketing for Voice of Vashon. He and his wife Susan moved from Miami to Vashon 'temporarily' in 1989 and live in the Lisabeula neighborhood.

ABOUT THE EDITOR

Alice Bloch is author of the memoirs *Mother-Daughter Banquet* and *Lifetime Guarantee* and the novel *The Law of Return*. She reviews opera and theater for Seattle Gay News and coordinates the Meals on Wheels program on Vashon Island, where she lives with her spouse and their two dogs.